LIVING-DEATH
TO
HONORED-LIFE

SEASONS
OF TRANSITIONS
FOR PARENTS
OF ASCENDED
CHILDREN

PRAISE FOR *LIVING-DEATH TO HONORED-LIFE*

I love Cynthia's unique approach in using the four seasons as an introspective guide for traversing and transforming the grief parents of ascended children experience. It truly is revolutionary in empowering parents to transition from the most painful life experience one can imagine, to one of honoring the life of their beloved child. Cynthia's memoir *"LIVING-DEATH TO HONORED-LIFE"* is a life journey filled with the shared love between parent and child, bringing forth a sacred, ritualistic practice by which the parent holds the skills and confidence to emerge from the dark abyss of their grief into the wholeness that promises an honored legacy entwined with their child's. If you are looking for a way to transform your grief into a deeper connection with your child, Cynthia's memoir shows you the path back to your heart and the love that brings you back to life again, and again.

—Sunny Dawn Johnston

Psychic Medium, Speaker, Teacher

Author: *The Love Never Ends: Messages From the Other Side*

www.sunnydawnjohnston.com

There are some people who know how to put words to what feels wordless, and direction when you are in a directionless place. Cynthia is one of those people, who has put into words; Remedies, Ideas, and Directions, as she takes you through the Seasons of grief. As a mother with a Child in Spirit, I know what the void feels like, and how even the smallest of tasks feel impossible - until they are possible again. Cynthia's wisdom guides the shattered heart, gently and honestly. She takes your hand and says, "This way, I got you."

I have read countless books in the five years, seven months, and zero days since my son ascended to Spirit. I have gained my own philosophy in the process. Yet, as I read through these pages, another level of understanding was opened to me. The Earth, her seasons, and This Unimaginable path were given new light and perspective. I could see clearly where I had been, where I was, and where I was going, and that all three of these parts are intertwined and coexist simultaneously, as we navigate this Mystical and Sacred Journey.

This is more than a memoir, it is a resource of wisdom to reference as you travel through your personal seasons of transitions, from what we know is living death, to the honored life of our children and for our children in Spirit. To the honored life of Ourselves.

—Raina Irene
Heart, Soul Spirit Practitioner, Poet, Oracle, Sacred Mommaz
Author: *Because of Josiah, The Sacred Alchemy of a Mother's Unending Bond with Her Son In Spirit.*
www.rainairene.love

I had the privilege of witnessing Cynthia Eyer go through the changes now chronicled in this book, shifting from what she calls the "death-in-life" of a long-grieving mother to a form of life-affirming universal motherhood that can care for the whole world. She offers useful insights on how to deal with grief with help from nature's cycles, and a vital reminder to trust our subtle "intuitive nudges" when they arise.

—Dr. Tina Fields PhD,
Director and Associate Professor,
Ecopsychology, Naropa University
Writer and Author
www.indigenize.wordpress.com

LIVING-DEATH TO HONORED-LIFE

SEASONS
OF TRANSITIONS
FOR PARENTS
OF ASCENDED
CHILDREN

CYNTHIA EYER

Living-Death to Honored-Life: Seasons of Transitions for Parents of Ascended Children

Copyright © 2023. Cynthia Eyer

ISBN: 979-8-9885147-1-8

Book Design by Transcendent Publishing
www.transcendentpublishing.com

First Edition, Transcendent Publishing, 2023

DISCLAIMER: This publication is meant as a source of valuable information for the reader; however, it is not intended to diagnose, treat, cure, or prevent any condition, nor is it meant as a substitute for direct expert assistance. If such level of assistance is required, the reader should seek out the services of a competent professional. The author holds a graduate degree in Transcendental EcoPsychology and does not hold a counseling license in any state or country. The following is a recreation of the events, experiences, and practices that assisted the author with her own sorrow and transcendence from her Living-Death to Honored-Life. She shares her mental, emotional, and psychological analysis to help others understand their own journeys through such practices and strategies. The results will differ for each individual; therefore the author makes no guarantees concerning the level of success anyone may experience. Again, these practices are not intended as a substitute for consultation with a licensed practitioner. Please consult with your own physician or healthcare specialist regarding the suggestions and recommendations made in this book. The use of this book implies your acceptance of this disclaimer.
Printed in the United States of America.

I dedicate my memoir to my son,
John Shawn Callahan II
03/27/1980 – 09/21/2003

"The only easy day
was
yesterday."

—Navy Seal Motto

TABLE OF CONTENTS

IN THE BEGINNING
THERE IS DARKNESS

When you are joyous, look deep into your heart
and you shall find
It is only that which has given you sorrow
that is giving you joy.
When you are sorrowful look again in your heart,
and you shall see
That in truth you are weeping
for that which has been your delight.

—Kahlil Gibran

I t's 20 September 2003, and the hurricane that hit Virginia Beach, Virginia had just crashed a huge tree behind my son's home. John and I were on the phone at the time, and he told me that he was going to check on the crash. He ran out in his shorts in the dark of night and saw the huge limb of the massive oak split and laying on his roof. He saw his neighbor come out, also in his shorts, to check on the crash and John, and they laughed, grateful it didn't completely take out the back of his home, grateful that all were safe. John, always the optimist.

Before we ended our call, he'd told me that he needed me to remain stationed in California. He didn't care where, he just wanted to be close to "Home" – meaning me. You see, we'd had to live apart since he was almost seventeen years old. I was in the Army, and in 1996 got stationed in South Korea, then in Florida after my unaccompanied tour, rather than being reassigned back to Colorado where he was finishing his senior year of high school and taking pre-college courses in physics. Every time we visited each other I was reminded of how much my own "Home" resided in my heart with my son's love. Our bond was especially strong since I had divorced his father when he was two years old.

When John first signed into the Navy, he asked me what his Rate (job) should be. He already knew he wanted to be part of that elite force, the Navy SEALS, so I asked him what he wanted to be for his SEALS team. His choice of Rate, I said, should reflect that desire. Without hesitation, and with his trademark mischievous smile, he said, "I love to blow shit up, Mom!" He chose Aviation Ordinance. He had a dark blue Navy Ordinance Division shirt with the words, "If you see me running…try and keep up," across the back in bright yellow lettering.

I have that shirt now.

I have read many books for parents whose child has ascended. I choose the word "*ascended*" because it seems a softer, kinder choice to me in seeing my Son, a warrior, in Valhalla awaiting for my own death to join him. In all those books I read and groups I attended, not one offered me ways to cope, traverse my own journey, and emerge from the dark abyss of my grief with a desire to live for him and myself. Not one offered or afforded me ways to emerge from my own living-death. Not one even recognized that I had died to the person I was and, in fact, no longer "was" after my son's ascension. I was just existing because my joy was no more. *Living-Death to Honored-Life* assists parents of ascended children, and those who support them, in learning how to cope with that which will remain within the deepest recesses of their hearts, emerging from their own living death into a life well-honored for them and their child.

When I chose the school at which to pursue my master's in psychology, I chose from a place of that death, wanting – needing – to get back to the land of the living so I could honor my son by living for the both of us. I learned, not only about how the seasons could help me understand my journey from living-death to honored-life, but how to relate those seasons and their in-between spaces relative to where I was at any given point in that journey (Foster & Little, 2005). Each season teaches me the depth of my humanness, and all aspects of those seasons are guides to and for me along the way. Each season and in-between space is a threshold into and through the fierce, stormy landscapes I traveled, while simultaneously healing me. The elements of each of the seasons teach me how to cope with the turmoil that rages inside of me as I move from the chaos and destruction to the eye of each storm, so I could look out and actually "see" what my truth was in the moment and embrace the calm that inevitably follows.

My Transpersonal EcoPsychology degree offered me insight into the fragments of my mental, emotional, and psychological states in which I found myself, within each season and liminal spaces between seasons. I began to tear down the elements taught in the psychology of the seasons and liminal spaces, and understand how those elements apply to my situation as a parent, especially a single parent whose only child has ascended and left her utterly alone. I learned how to use the seasons to cope with the fact that I will never be able to pick up the shattered shards turned to ashes. I cannot "re-create." I must be reborn from my own living-death, emerging from the dark, desolate, isolated, bitter, dissonant landscapes, filled with the stink of rotting ground, and "create" my Self anew. I must learn for myself so I can offer a purpose beyond my own life, one that honors my son's life. I must learn to cultivate seeds of gratitude for what was and now is, from a place of hope fed by love instead of loss fed by fear.

I have always been used by The Divine as a catalyst for change for others' greater good. I write this book as a catalyst for your own change. I write this book to cultivate the seeds of gratitude for what was and now is in each of your own lives. No one can be for us what we need. We, as parents of ascended children, must learn to be for ourselves what we need to emerge from our living-death into an honored-life for our child within the life of ourselves. I write this book from my own experiences and how I learned the processes that showed me how to cope with them and emerge into my truth of who I am now. Even after nearly two decades, I continue to learn how to use the seasons of my humanness to navigate those land-scapes and use the time I have left in a way that honors my son's life, our life together, and my life on my own. The greatest gift we can offer our children is to honor their legacies through living who they were while they were here. I honor John's legacy within me by choosing an honorary life as impactful as his ascension was for me.

Within each chapter are my own stories, told as examples of the mental, emotional, psychological, spiritual, and physical transitions I underwent to take the next step, the next breath. There are also interactive, experiential activities that you will want to go back to so you can discover, in your own time and understanding, what it feels like, looks like, smells like, tastes like, and sounds like to touch the joy of your child in the life within your life, and not their ascension. In the back pages of this guide you will find sections on terminology and other resources to assist you in your journey from a Living-Death to an Honored-Life. There is an offering of a *Life Journal* that one can record their experiences when interacting with the experiential activities in the book, as well as revelations for oneself. It is an accompaniment to this book, as well as it's own form of healing for oneself. As one emerges through the seasons, each transition is a practice of the heart, mind, body, and Soul. So, get what you need to mark your pages and passages, and bring your journals so you can record your own stories and experiences. Wherever the emerging revelations may take you is where you need to be in that season.

This book is your gift to yourself and your child. Allow it to move you in ways other experiences have not. Allow your own experiences within the pages to help you discover the next step, the next breath from your place of darkness, returning and emerging reborn into the light of your life, as the light of your child.

Welcome to your Self, your Truth, Who You Are Now, and Who You Are to Become. Breathe in the love from the Divine. In the space between breathing in and breathing out, hold gratitude for who you are in this moment and gratitude for the breath that continues to offer you the gift which honors your child. Breathe out and offer that gift, with gratitude drenched in your love for your child, to the world. Enter your breath and know thyself. Enter your season where you are right now, your human-ness, and become your Truth – each and every breath, every moment, every day. The seasons are your way back home, back to your heart, back to the seat of your Soul, back to your deepest, most rewarding love that transcends death, again and again.

BREATHE

FROM THE FULLNESS OF LIFE
TO
A LIVING-DEATH

Please allow me to share my story of how I experienced John's ascension. You no doubt have your own story of that moment when you knew your child had left the physical world. I would be honored if you shared your story with me. I have my own confidential website link and a group for parents of ascended children that you are welcome to join and comment within. I have found, within my own bachelor's and graduate degree programs in psychology and coaching sessions with other women, that groups offer us so many benefits. In these safe places, we can share our processes and be witnessed as we witness others. We support each other in loving kindness, embracing our transitional experiences with grace, and honoring our humanity. My story also tells you a little about who I was (key here is *was*), the relationship I shared with my son, and how the one moment changed everything.

On 20 September 2003, the storm of the hurricane's eye that battered the eastern border of Virginia left much destruction in its wake. An ominous foretelling of what was to still occur within my own life. The storm cleared that night, and the next afternoon John and one of his best friends, Marc Lee, with whom he was going through the first phase of B.U.D.S. (Basic Underwater Demolition

SEALS), and their SEAL Trainer, Bryan Bill, decided to go on a motorcycle ride. Grandfather Sun was shining bright and promising the perfect day for such an event after being cooped up for three days. For a twenty-three-year-old young man who held a passion for life, John took every opportunity to get to be outside and live it to its (and his) fullest. We both did. He also saw himself as everyone's protector, regardless of who they were in his circle. He insisted on taking the lead.

I was stationed in Victorville, California, the opposite side of our worlds together. I saw my position in the Army as a stewardship, one of creating, raising up, and maintaining the Soldiers of four detachment units. My mission was always to keep my Soldiers safe at all times, mitigating the chances of a fatal incident through training them. If I failed them in this stewardship, I had failed them in life. So, I trained them with real-life scenarios, pyro techniques, and helicopter airlifts included. We had so much fun learning the tough stuff. My son always insisted that if we couldn't have fun (translated as our Souls giggling with the joy of it and what it brought to others) doing the tough stuff, the tough stuff wasn't worth doing.

I and the soldiers of the detachments, together, were on a forced march with all our battle-rattle, walking the desert sands on patrol missions, encountering the different training scenarios we would experience together in war. As a strong, athletic, competitive individual, I took to heart what I trained others in and never expected anything from them I wasn't willing, or capable of doing myself. That was John's way as well. It's how we cared for others, by helping them learn to be great fishers, cultivating an ability to rise above what they thought possible. We started out at 5:00 a.m., for in September the heat in the desert could get unbearable, especially when the sand added to the reflective heat of the sun. The desert also offers us psychological conditioning, finding within our internal landscapes the life-preserving qualities so we can bear and overcome the malignant external landscapes we sometimes are required to serve in. Unbeknownst to me, this was about to become my internal landscape for some time.

Somewhere around 4:30 a.m., my intuitive guidance kept encouraging me to call my son before we started the march, just to say hello and that I love him. We never hung up with each other, or our friends and family, without saying (and meaning), "I love you." Even if we had a strong disagreement, we never left each other's side until we talked it out, even if it was 3:00 in the morning and we both had to be at work at o-dark-thirty. That was our pact and the strength of our love for each other and those in our circle.

I wasn't thinking straight, for on that morning of 21 September 2003, my thoughts were on all that needed to be accomplished in the next two days of training; my heart was at the ready to prepare these sacred Soldiers for what is inevitable for so many of them. I misjudged, thinking that John and I were in the same time zone and it was too early to call, being that we had been on the phone rather late (or should I say early, as it was well past 1 a.m.)the night before. In fact, John was in Virginia, three hours ahead. I guess I was more tired than I was willing to accept and admit. My Soldiers couldn't see any vulnerabilities in their leader, always the stoic as their example to serve by. That stoicism extended to my own humanity, never accepting any excuse for a miss-step. I miss-stepped gravely that morning by not listening to my inner push to call him.

During the last fifteen minutes of the four-hour-plus forced march, I felt this great surge of energy enter me, like I could feel everything in the Universe and nothing at all. I didn't have any human needs or desires present in my body, mind, or heart. I couldn't feel my body anymore, my boots hitting the desert ground, the heat radiating off my skin, the sweat pouring down and soaking my uniform, the weight of the battle-rattle bearing down on my neck, shoulders, and back. I couldn't hear anything, and yet every human sense was enhanced. Then everything in my consciousness went dark. Although my body was continuing on automatic in the living realm, I wasn't really there. It was like my Soul had left my body and was watching the picture movie of my life in that moment. I had no human need or urge to sit, walk, stand, talk, see, hear, eat, drink, sleep, or even breathe. My Soul left my human shell and merged with this unspeakable, unfathomable peace beyond what was (and still is), humanly comprehensible. It was like watching a hologram of myself – there, but not there.

Some of my soldiers watched me with worried brows, knowing something wasn't quite right. They expressed their concern, saying that in the two years they had completed training scenarios with me they had never seen me stumble, waver, and falter like they were witnessing now. I viewed them with puzzlement, not knowing what they spoke of. I ordered lunch, even though I still felt no human requirements for life. Lunch went untouched. I was flanked by two very close friends in the unit and in my life, both intensely watching me in silence.

After training was complete, three of my section Soldiers told me to go home and they would finish up and lock up. I didn't even think to squash that, as I was always the first one in and the last one out. I didn't feel the need, for even my ego was absent. I drove my best friend, Evelyn, to her home and went to leave for my own. I didn't get out of the parking lot when the phone rang. It was my ex-husband. What the hell was he calling me for? We hadn't spoken in over six years and how the hell did he get my phone number! I asked him as much and he said, with a shaky voice, "John was in an accident and declared DOA."

Instantly, a storm as merciless as the one that had battered John's external world the previous three days, hit me full force. I was in the depths of the storm, being battered and torn asunder. My very Being, the essence of my joy, had shattered into a trillion pieces. My life as I had known it was nothing but powder and shards of glass gouging me. It felt like the house I had built within me was swept up, splintering every picture, every smile, every joy that my son and I shared in our twenty-three years together. My hopes and dreams for him, his legacy of all the wonderful essence he is, my own legacy through him and his children and their children – who would never be – fragmented out of me, exploding into the ethereal darkness of nothingness. There existed no light within me. No discernment of the life I once knew and lived with my son. The moment my son ascended, I also did. I had just entered my own death – my Living-Death – and I couldn't breathe. I gasped for air without any filling my lungs. I screamed without sound, cried without tears, crushed into the fine powder of the broken panes through which my heart used to view our life together.

The automated self that had been driving since she was fifteen years old put the car in park where it was, turned the ignition off, and walked back to Evelyn's home. I couldn't tell her because I was still screaming without sound. I finally collapsed on my knees, balling myself up into the same shape as a baby in the womb. I had died when he took his last breath, my Soul ascending with him to carry him back to The Divine. I must have stayed in the realm of Spirit with John until that call from his father, for no human requirement entered back into me until that very moment. The rush, like molten lava, flowed over me, and I was powerless to stop it, struggling to breathe as it crushed me under the burning weight of my living-death.

I had just entered the Winter Season and I would remain there until I learned how to cope with my grief and sorrow through seeing my life within each season and the transitions with and between them. Nineteen years have passed since that fatal day, and there are still times I feel like I am back in the moment I first learned the truth of my son's ascension; I'm back in the womb – alive and not yet alive knowing life. My breath stops and moments pass before my body automatically takes over and I return to the now, my lungs filling with air as my breath hitches to reach deeply within the recesses of my heart. This is the life of a parent of an ascended child. There is no denying it. Yet now we have hope and a way to transition into a space by which we offer ourselves more grace with honor, so we may honor our child's life that lives on within us with more grace.

We cannot be for someone else what we are not willing to be for ourselves, for there is nothing to offer. We also cannot make anyone else think, say, feel, or do anything. We think, say, feel, and do because we think and feel that is what we want, and need, for our greater good in that moment. This becomes our truth, not another's. After the ascension of our child, this is almost always someone else's truth at our expense. It is the need for us to be a certain way for them because they don't know how to be for us – or themselves. Their well-meaning is their blindness and their blindness is the darkness of fear that they aren't what you need. They create their own need and project it as our truth – our belief. When we change our belief, we change what we know. When we change what we know – an intimate, active, interactive relationship in our heart-mindset – we change our truth.

I wake up every day since asking The Divine to just help me breathe and to honor my son by continuing to live in my truth, not what others expect of me. My first three years after John's ascension are almost a blank blur, without much memory. Every day was the struggled grappling of not driving off the road or bridge into the water that awaited, beckoning me to rush to the water I was already drowning in. The watery grave that existed within me from the tears flowing from and rushing out of the darkness of my joyless heart. The watery grave I still find myself emerging from, gasping for the air that I promised to keep breathing so I can honor my son through the life he asked me to live for him. These are the moments of each transformational transition that every parent must enter when their child ascends. For a single-parent of an only child, the pain feels exponentially worse to me and takes on a greater significance. My son was my legacy and I reveled in his life as a reflection of my own. My joy was my son because his joy was making a gift of himself that he offered others. That joy was ripped out of me, an explosion of bone, organs, tissue, and sinew that left only a burnt, empty husk I no longer recognized – nor wanted. I was a dried, desolate shell of my former self.

I felt as if the home John and I had played in, chasing each other with cups of dishwater as we laughed and teased each other, living a life that resonated with the joy of our mother-son love, had erupted like a volcano, its fiery lava flow now crushing down upon me. The image of the lava flowing over me and encapsulating me in a living-death flooded me with panic. I was panicking at the thought that I was, and still am, helpless to save my son.

In time, I came to understand that to honor my son I must learn to re-engage with all that he was, and is, and carry that forth into my own life. I must leave the wasteland and find within my internal landscape that which offers and affords me "living waters" so my life will hold purpose for us both. I am the source of life for us both. My lava tomb had become my lava egg. I would enter the stages from a living-death to where the seed in the lava egg would originate into who I was in each moment – once again to be a babe. I had been readying myself to be reborn and emerge from the in-between of death and life all those years since. I witnessed, and still witness, the four seasons that each emergence took – the four seasons and their transitional phases of our humanness and the essence of self in each element of those seasons and transitional phases.

The seasons are windows by which you witness your own transition. As you read one passage, one paragraph, one story, one page, your life transitions from who you were to who you are in that moment. Each transition is another star that illuminates your deeper Self in your own lava tomb. As you turn the page, a dawning is witnessed within yourself, revealing the internal landscape you currently are experiencing, offering you an opportunity to find the life-giving waters. Each experience shows you the seasons of your own humanness within that experience and how your trajectory between those seasons is either stifling you – depriving you of your honor for you and your child – or transmuting and shifting you into your greater Self with a grace that honors both you and your child.

Each passage, paragraph, story, page, and experience offered in this book offers you a way to cope with your own grief and transitions you into the seasons of your humanness. The seasons show you the path back to your own truth, offering you an intimate, active, interactive, heart-mind relationship with yourself. As you follow this path, you offer yourself the ability to emerge from your Living-Death and live fully in honor of yourself and your child. Each transition is an awakening, a dawning to who you are now. Each dawning brings forth an opportunity to awaken to your birth and each birth brings you into a new unfolding of who you are in that moment. Each season offers you an option to either stay in that season or learn from it in that moment and transition to the next.

Over the past three days I have been experiencing anxiety attacks as I prepare myself to descend into the depths and befriend the forces that keep me stoic while writing this book. I wake every morning re-minding my SELF, my Soul to my heart, so I can offer myself my humanity and write. I look inside to see that I'm back in my Child Season, starting my life all over again and asking Spirit to show me how I breathe into my day and my life. The Child Season allows me to feel what my body is sharing with me through its language.

Turn the page into your own transition within and through each of the four seasons, revealing your humanness in each. The inner Babe of your rebirth awaits you, and with it the joy of your child, in your child, within your emergence in life for you both, into an honored-life.

SEASONS
OF A
LIVING-DEATH
TO AN
HONORED-LIFE

INTRODUCTION TO
THE
FOUR SEASONS
AND
TRANSFORMATIONAL PHASES

"And God said, 'Let there be lights in the expanse of the heavens to separate the day from the night. And let them be for signs and for seasons, and for days and years, and let them be lights in the expanse of the heavens to give light upon the earth.

And it was so. And God made the two great lights – the greater light to rule the day and the lesser light to rule the night."

—Genesis 1:14-17

There are two lights and four seasons all parents will transition through in the continuous cycle of rebirth we all experience after our child ascends. There is the light that was our child's life in our life and the light in our darkness by which we traverse our journey that is now our path. Our journey holds many changes through recognizing the course of movement, development, and awareness. In those changes exist the four seasons in our process, which offer us seeds by which we cultivate an emergence of new life to honor our self and our child. Within those cultivated seeds we birth ways to cope within the many stages of our grief until we transition into a life that holds meaning, transforming ourselves within each season. We learn how to live an honored-life moving forward into something more meaningful, with a richer intuitive sense of purpose.

The four seasons are internal seasons of our mind, psyche, heart, body, and soul which manifest in our external landscapes of our life as choices. I will introduce each of the seasons and the transitional phases, explaining in greater detail how each element and symbol comforts, guides, and advises one on their journey. Each parent transitions from their death of who they were to the discovery of who they are, into the birth of who they are to become, cultivated within each season. I choose the word "cultivated" because the seasons are seeds that are planted within each phase of each parent's journey, and it is up to each parent to find the light that nourishes those seeds. Those seeds become the conception of who we will become, how we choose to show up, so that our life is filled with more grace, honoring our human self and our spiritual Self in the journey. I capitalize the spiritual Self to emphasize our connection with The Divine. We are on this journey for the rest of our human lives, seeking to find meaning beyond our experience of our living-death so we can cope and emerge as a benefactor of the love of our child that brings us back to them in life again and again. This is our pledge to our child that each of us can commit to.

Later in the book we will discuss how the seasons comfort, guide, and advise us in the different areas of one's life that are impacted and how others can support us, not only on our journey but theirs as well. All who are close to us and our child are affected by their ascension. It is imperative that they understand their own transitions through time in order to gain a deeper, greater understanding of a parent's transitions through time. Again, we can never hope to be for another what we have not learned for ourselves. We cannot offer a Soul a drink from the Living-Well if the well is not known to us. That knowing is the active, interactive relationship supporters have with themselves in their own transition.

In "knowing," we then begin to seek within ourselves the answers we desire and need to aid us in our journey. Jesus tells us to "seek and ye shall find." To find, we must begin at the beginning – our living-death in the Winter Season – where we are swallowed up and thrust into the darkness of the abyss that is the sorrow and grief that has taken residence in the deepest recesses of our heart. From there, we move through the seasons of our Soul, where we seek refuge: our Child Season where rebirth takes place, the Adolescent Season where our emotions inform us, and back to the Season of our Heart. It is only when we recognize our Self experiencing our human self in each transition within and through the seasons that we find the heaven that is the joy of our child. For joy is the essence of heaven and heaven is the birth of joy. As children of The Divine, we reach for the arms that wrap us in the fullness of love. We reach for the arms of our Divine Mother and Father and so touch the arms of our child, receiving their love again, and again, and again.

Everyone begins at the beginning. So let us begin.

SEASON OF THE HEART
BETWEEN
LIFE AND A LIVING-DEATH

*"Memories saturate my heart and
the story of you spills from my eyes."*

—Grace Andren

The Season of Life in a Living-Death symbolizes:

The Death of the Adult That Was

Heart and Community

The Heart's Grief Received in the Body and Mind

The Dark Bitterness of a Season in Winter

Order & Death of What No Longer Serves

Age of the Wise Elder

The Eros of Love for Self and Others

Rest and Restoration

The Direction of North

The Element of Earth

> *Two weeks before that fatal day on 21 September 2003, I told a*
> *small group of Soldiers who were, and still are, very close to me*
> *that if my son every died before me they would need to put me in*
> *a locked room, medicated to keep from ending my own life, for*
> *Johnny was my very Light that exists as my Soul. He was my*
> ***Heart.***

The Winter Season symbolizes the death of life as we know it, the darkness of this season being the seeming entirety of our existence. On 21 September 2003, I entered the bitter darkness of the Winter Season, where my heart exploded into the deepest, most intense sorrow that grief can ever take one. My heart no longer wanted to beat, for it no longer could feel the rhythm that was me and John. Every breath I took was an act of God and the Angels. The loving harmonious energies of my heart's experiences with John were beyond shattered, and the very existence of who I was in those experiences was no more. The life tether that connected me and my son had been palpable in my heart's energy center. The harmonious vibrations which played in my entire being since his birth was the music of my Soul. Now that tether had been severed; the music was silent, and I was devoid of all hope for life. Internally, the landscape I related my entire being in was the familiar, full darkness of the icy, frozen tundra of Alaska. I knew this darkness well, as I had been stationed there for a year and two months after my son was born. The darkness, to me, was maleficent in its nature, yet offering me prophetic insight in the midst of my interminable darkness. Psychologically, a parent can experience persistent seasonal affective disorder (SAD) without any construct of time. Each parent of an ascended child experiences their immediate landscapes differently. My own persistent SAD lasted for many years before I was ready to sit with my darkness and find the prophetic gems it held for me so I could emerge and transition into the season of Spring. "Ready" isn't an expectation of the human self; it's a calling from one's Self – one's Soul.

The Winter Season signifies the Heart's grief in the body, as the body holds memory reflexes of past traumatic experiences. Scientifically, the heart is the physiological energy center of our very existence. Its vibrational energy is the harmony by which all other energy centers interact from. We now know that the heart has its own neurological centrum, receiving messages in the body from the sixth and seventh sensory perception axes. The heart then sends these messages as coded vibrations, simultaneously, to the body and the brain. The brain then mirrors those vibrational messages as active/reactive conditionings to the body and emotional centers of the brain. In essence, the body receives the same conditioning as the emotional centers of the brain. This is how, according to Dr. Bessel van der Kolk, author of *The Body Keeps the Score: The Brain, Mind and Body in the Healing of Trauma* (2015), the body holds the memories of all experiences and acts/reacts according to the similarities, times, and/or conditions of current experiences. To offer an example, how many of us feel a grave sense of doom in our body around the date of our child's ascension, perhaps waking in the midst of a panic attack, prior to our mind registering the body's vibrational messages? The heart energy center is reliving that traumatic experience as a memory and sending those vibrational messages to the body as a response to the experience. Dr. Gregg Braden, in his April 12, 2020, talk titled "The Ancient Technique to Making Tough Decisions," discusses this same physiological phenomenon.

The heart energy center remembers the very moment we experienced our child's ascension, and in that moment, our own death of who we were. The heart center remembers and stores that moment and what that felt like, looked like, smelled like, tasted like, and sounded like, internally and externally. Mothers experience their child's ascension differently than fathers experience it. It isn't better or worse, it's just different. It is important to honor the differences in those experiences and that sometimes those differences will not always be understood. We will all enter a stage that is filled with both internal anger and bargaining conversations. Anger that our child, our reason and purpose for our heart's and Soul's very existence, is no longer with us, and the internal conversations around bargaining with The Divine in what-if scenarios, followed by regrets for the loss of those what-ifs scenarios. It is only human nature to seek out someone we can blame for our Winter Season's darkness, devoid of all existence. Be that The Divine or another human, we seek out an entity to scream to in the void of the abyss that is us. Psychologically, parents enter the stage of anger and bargaining from a place of guilt fed by our sense of hopelessness. We feel in our body the hopelessness of being able to keep our child safe. I always understood that I was a steward over the gift of my Son from The Divine. I entrusted Them to keep him safe. The Divine was who I screamed to in my abyssal void. They were my anger and my bargaining chip as to why and how I would go on living when no parent should ever live beyond their child.

For me, survivor's guilt set in right away. How do I have the right, and the rite, to go on living, when such a promising Old Soul was taken at such a very young age? Why was his loving and caring life that filled so many with such joy worth less than mine? How do I go on in this physical realm? The air in my lava shell suffocated me, the darkness a constant reminder that I had been forgotten by the Divine. Our Lord-Goddess had forsaken me and left me to die, while not allowing me to die. They encaged me in this living-death, a withered lifeform abandoned in her shell. I felt betrayed. Soon the crows would come and devour what was left of my light in John – my memories of the life lived with my son. The crows had something else planned.

My story around my sense of not being able to keep my son safe was that the Angels kept wanting me to call him that day, yet for some reason my mind was mistakenly thinking that it was too early, when actually, he was in a time zone three hours ahead. I reasoned that "IF" I had called John would I have delayed him, and he would still be alive because of that delay. In reality, if I had called him, it would have made no difference in the time. I just would have had the blessing to be able to speak to him one last time before he ascended. I was offered an intuitive gift and I didn't listen. I learned from this experience to stop and listen when The Divine gives me an intuitive nudge. I don't dismiss it, and in being more aware of my intuitive states I am blessed beyond expression with other loved ones.

When the crows did come on the battlefield of my heart, I heard the voice of my precious son telling me to not drive off the bridge or walk out into the water and breathe in deeply its contents. He would come like an Angel and ask me to not give up our love to the wasteland I was currently experiencing. He would call me in those darkest of moments and ask me to not dishonor our life we had together. The Divine was gently sharing Their love for me, as They did for those eight months before his ascension, reminding me that They had not forsaken me, and that John had pre-ordained to go back to the Light of Them at that moment. That John's human death held a greater purpose than it appeared. That this was John's decision, his chosen destiny, all in his Soul's knowing that his buddies, Marc and Bryan, were destined for much greater lives – and in turn touch more lives – than any of us were aware of in that moment. That both John and I were catalysts for greater change, beyond who we were and are. All would be revealed in time.

The Season of Winter symbolizes the internal and external landscapes of the darkest, coldest realms which hold no life, light, or hope of recovery. Or so it seems. The Winter landscapes are both a place to die from that which no longer serves us and a place for restoration. They hold both a darkness and a light of revelation. The days are shorter, the nights longer, and so the conversations are more from the heart. Winter, in the landscape of community, is where all look to each other for comfort and companionship. Community can be family, friends, co-workers, and/or pets. Community can be external landscapes, such as an indoor greenhouse, a grove of oaks, a frozen creek bed, or a group of like-hearted others who seek nourishment from each other. The season of Winter is about going into our own darkness and sitting down with a shot or a cuppa and befriending who we are in the darkness. That friendship offers us the gift of revealing who and what keeps us small and who and what offers us the gift of light. The gifts of light we allow ourselves reveal the gifts our darkness harbors for us. What happens *to* us is our *fate* and what we choose to be from our fate is what becomes our **destiny**. Winter shows us that life is fleeting and so how do we choose to *be* in life, with life, for life so that our life is purposefully in honor of ourselves and the life of our child through us. External Winter landscapes help us to see how they serve us in our restoration.

External Winter landscapes aid us in recognizing how we find nourishment within our different communities as we bustle around the hearth to feel both the warmth of the fire and the warmth of others. Do we not look to hastily enter the coziness of shops and others' homes to escape the bitterness of the cold? Do we not seek cozy foods and warming drinks to nourish not only our bodies but our hearts and minds? Winter landscapes ask us, they beckon us to go inward to find the reserves that reside for healing and restoration. They communicate with us how what appears to be suspended in barren, inhospitable existence, is a place of solitude to retreat inward and rest. Do the trees, barren to the bones of their trunks and limbs, seemingly void of life while carrying the weight of snow storms, shattered limbs beyond repair from the storm, not begin to reach for the light of Spring and bloom, reborn into full glory in the Summer? This is who each parent is upon the ascension of their child and who they will remain until they are restored enough to transition into the season of Spring.

As mentioned, the internal Winter landscape I found myself in was like that of the Alaskan frozen tundra drenched in eternal darkness. The breath was frozen upon my body as I attempted to breathe. There was no life and there was no light. I could not tell you much of what was experienced in the first three years after John ascended. The external surroundings of my home and office were outward manifestations of who I was internally. I am a very neat person with a place for everything and everything in its place. Those surroundings were a cluster of all I had collected and was, scattered everywhere. I attempted to make some semblance of order, flitting from one project to another, one area to another, one idea to another. Disarray, confusion, lack of patience, intolerance, frustration, protection, and fear ruled; chaos reigned, with no room for compassion.

The external landscape of my home was littered with dark colors and I felt "homeless." I didn't recognize the energy that existed within myself and thus my outer surroundings. Because I couldn't recognize, as yet, the healing the Winter Season offers, I attempted to disguise my internal Winter with decorations of Spring and filled my internal Winter with "projects" and work. I looked forward to going to work so I could escape a life without my deeper, more intimate purpose and calling. I struggled to find my Divine purpose in the world without my son, and so I plunged myself into the calling of others. Everyone's *purpose* is to remember that they are born of The Divine, from The Divine of love, for love, and to be love in the Universe. One's *calling* is how they choose to be that love in, and for, the Universe. Other Soldiers' lives and the mission for the Unit became my raft on the waters ravaged by the storm that was in me, thus becoming both my purpose and my calling. I "created" hope for others, or so I thought. I made Soldiers' lives my life so I could feel like I held validity in a life I wasn't supposed to be living. This was supposed to be my son's life and I was supposed to be the one who had ascended.

The light in that darkness came when I realized that I bought a lot of things to create beautiful life images where all I perceived was the obscurity of life, a façade. I created beautiful floral arrangements, painted the dining room a luminous teal, covered old furniture in floral prints with floral throw pillows, placed an assortment of tropical plants in the TV room with hammock seating hung from the ceiling beams and chiffon materials wrapped the windows, framing them in exotic colors. I tried to externally decorate my internal winterscape with other worlds because I couldn't accept who and where I was in this living-death world I was simply existing in. As I emotionally, mentally, and psychologically ran from my internal winterscape, I found my internal scape was being manifested within the moving from state to state as the Army moved me from one assignment to the next. I was psychologically urging the time to quicken.

I wasn't aware I was traversing a living-death in the dark, frigid landscape of the Alaskan Winter.

When I learned of the seasons as partners for my journey, the light in my darkness became the lights of the aurora borealis, cast when the conditions were just right. I was ready to sit in my darkness with a shot of Jameson or a cuppa and befriend her. I was ready to mine the Earth and find the gems the darkness held for me. I was ready to be in awe and wonder of the aurora borealis and allow it to dance in my heart, the seat of my Soul, with my son. I was ready to stay in the North until I was strong enough to transition.

The season of Winter symbolizes the cold found in the Northern Hemisphere. It becomes the direction that is assimilated when we want to orientate ourselves to our surroundings. It's the direction of endings and beginnings. It's the direction of the liminal space between life and death and death into seed. North is the direction most do not wish to travel, for the North represents loss in the experience of grief which resonates with the Season of Fall. Because others don't know how to "be" with us anymore, our living-death is exponentially lonelier in the darkness of the North. We are cast into a profound depth of loss, all else the void we experience emotionally, psychologically, spiritually, and physically. We are flung into what is psychologically recognized as the Season of Anxiety Disorder. This disorder is very real, as the brain can no longer create the chemicals that assist with overcoming grief. It's okay to seek professional aide, even if that aide is a medication that helps our brain to create those chemicals. I seek holistic healing, without medicines, as much as possible. In this case, however, I knew that my brain would not create the chemicals needed to keep me functioning so I readily took a medicine so I could continue in the service required for the Army. I chose to listen to my son's voice so I could go on living as best I could for him.

I can't take those medicines now, because they affect me in ways that aren't healthy for me. Because my brain can now create the chemicals needed to aid me in feeling the Divine Love between myself and my son, the medicines are now a detriment to a condition I have had since birth known as generalized anxiety disorder (GAD) with panic attacks. When I was but ten days old I had pneumonia and died. Thankfully, I was revived, but the same thing happened a year later. Though I never died again after that, I continued to be afflicted with pneumonia every year until the age of six. Every year, after a period in the hospital, my parents were told to take me home and enjoy me, for I would not live out the winter. I later learned from Dr. Kolk's work that the panic attacks I experience are indeed my body's way of "keeping the score" of those death-defying moments stored in the heart's energy center. I still have panic attacks, just not so many and not so intense since using the seasons as guides and informants.

There are a few activities at the end of this chapter that assist me in grounding myself so I can gain a footing along my journey. In this, I look to Mother Earth to guide me and support me.

The Winter Season symbolizes the element of Earth, where we are stuck and unable to enter into the same realm as our child; yet, at the same time, it is the very ground by which we sow, germinate, and cultivate the seeds by which we seek the essence of who we are to become. The Earth is seemingly void of life, a scarcity that mirrors our inner landscape and fills us with fear. The fear of our inability to bring life back. We are the cocooned worm that has entered their stage of living-death, and like the emergence of the butterfly from its cocoon, the emergence holds great beauty and freedom for the honored-life that we are to become within the struggles of emergence. Winter is the inner landscape we struggle to emerge from.

The frozen landscape that we now inhabit, and that inhabits us, is the struggle with our darkest shadow of Self. We must take our pick in hand and dig deep into the frozen crust of the abyss until we uncover the gems that are buried deep within the recesses of our heart. As the gems are revealed, they shed illumination upon and within the darkness to help us rise against the darkness to forge a life of light for our Self (higher

Self) and our child. We forge so our living-death doesn't claim us for eternity, leaving our child's story untold. The forging for the light within our darkness is the fortitude we have to live on in the depths of our fear, the fortitude to live on for our child, and the fortitude to face the struggle to emerge from our grief.

Our fortitude is our mantle of courage to recognize our vulnerability during this season and continue to forage the Earth for the gems of light that penetrate our darkness. Without the foraging, there are no stories to share of our child, thus no continuation of their strength, smile, laughter, kindness, joy, and love that is them within us. Earth is where we descend so that we may sit with the darkness and speak with it so that we may understand it more deeply. It is this darkness of the wintered Earth that we begin to learn of the depths of what sorrow is for us. This isn't meant for anyone else. It is our own and it is unique to each. Spouses do not experience the same sorrow or darkness, nor do they traverse the same path on their journeys, for each is a unique Soul experiencing what it means to be a human in this journey of transition.

When we sit with our darkness and learn how to listen to its silent stillness, an illumination begins to reveal within us the light we need, and require, to live an honored-life. We begin to seek the deeper meaning, not only for ourselves but to rebuild a life that is an illumination of our child's very Soul, present on Earth. We seek the resounding love in the tether of our Soul joined with the Soul of our child. We seek to cultivate the love we had, and still have, with our child that brings us back to life again and again. The seeking is our transitional phase between the Winter Season of our living-death into the Spring Season of our Soul's reconnection with our child.

Here is a poem relevant to this season that has aided me.

Onto a Vast Plain
you are not surprised at the force of the storm—
you have seen it growing.

The trees flee. Their flight
sets the boulevards streaming. And you know:
He whom they flee is the one
you move toward. All your senses
sing him, as you stand at the window.

The weeks stood still in summer.
The trees' blood rose. Now you feel
it wants to sink back
into the source of everything. You thought
you could trust that power
when you plucked the fruit:
Now it becomes a riddle again,
and you again a stranger.

Summer was like your house: you knew
where each thing stood.
Now you must go out into your heart
as onto a vast plain. Now
the immense loneliness begins.
The days go numb, the wind
sucks the world from your senses like wintered leaves.

Through the empty branches the sky remains.
It is what you have.
Be earth now, and evensong.
Be the ground lying under the sky.
Be modest now, like a thing
ripened until it is real,
so that he who began it all
can feel you when he reaches for you.

– Rainer Maria Rilke

EXPERIENTIAL ACTIVITIES TO ASSIST TRANSITIONS BETWEEN WINTER'S HEART AND SPRING'S SOUL

1. **Professional Counseling:** Seek professional counseling and share the journal with the counselor. Ideally, you might seek a Jungian/Rogerian therapist, as these therapies are the most profound in assisting with each stage of emergence in grief. They assist one in seeing their own humanity in the journey of grief and recognizing the darkness and light of one's Self in that humanity. If we broke a bone we would seek medical attention and go through physical therapy. The heart, mind, body, and soul of a parent are crushed and must seek medical attention and follow through with psychological therapy to emerge into an honored-life for their child in Self.

2. **Group Therapy:** Group therapy is not always with a licensed therapist, nor is one required. Anyone can start their own group; in fact, I offer a group that meets monthly on zoom. You are welcome to join us. We all experience the pitfalls of our grief as an overwhelming, discouraging, judgmental sorrow from unrealistic, cultural, social, and economic expectations. Although offered or given with altruistic intentions, some advice from those who have never experienced our unique grief as a parent of an ascended child can derail us from our journey. Our grief isn't worse or better than another's, however, it is very different from other forms of loss.

   a. **Instills Hope:** *Psychology Today* states that one of the potential benefits of grief groups is that they instill hope in their members. Those in support groups are more able, and willing, to see themselves in different stages of their grief transition and transformation. Some members are in their acute phase and others are much further within their transition, while others are in their transformation phases. Each member is afforded the gift of witnessing where they are and where they seek to travel through the experiences of others. Our witnessing of Self and others offers us hope that we will be able to move forward in our own journey.

b. **Acceptance and Acclamation**: One of the greatest gifts we can receive from a like-hearted, universal group is acceptance of where we currently are in our grief and a safe environment in which we become acclimated to that place. Each phase, transition, and transformation is like a season that we must learn to acclimatize ourselves to. This group assists all members to learn the "temperature" and "season" they are in and with which to associate their feelings, thoughts, struggles, sorrows, joys, revelations, transitions, and transformations. When we feel totally alone, misunderstood, or ostracized by the world because the people in our world are frustrated by their own lack of understanding, the support in this group becomes the haven for understanding. This group not only facilitates support within the group; together, we learn how to help others to understand and support us outside of the group.

c. **Group Information Imparts Perspective and Wisdom**: Those members who possess a deeper wisdom within their own transitions and transformations are equipped to altruistically offer helpful insight, advice, rituals, practices, and understanding with compassion and empathy. The wisdom gained from our own experiences helps to lighten the load for others who are going or will go through similar experiences. This brings us back to our hope that we are not alone and that we too can experience something different from our current world. It is important to state that each experience is unique for each person. We all might be in our cocoons, yet our transitioning within our transformation is unique – not better or worse, just different.

d. **Group Cohesiveness**: All of the aforementioned benefits create a cohesive bond for each of the Group's Members. It is our human nature to want, to need, to belong. As single parents of an only child who has ascended, we feel like we no longer belong anywhere. We lose every form of identity that we have been told we are associated with. This sense of difference and isolation from social norms impacts our sense of happiness and well-being. This impact becomes our reality. The Group breaks the perceptive lens of this reality and shows us the way out of the darkness.

SEASON OF TETHERING
BETWEEN
HEART AND SOUL

"Our souls speak a language that is beyond human understanding.
A connection so rare the universe won't let us part."

—Nikki Rowe

The Soul Season symbolizes:

The Season of Spring

Spiritual Nourishment

The Miraculous Seed of Re-Birth

The Will of Divinity

Inspiration & Creativity

The Eye of The Divine

The Eros of Spiritual Love

The Direction of East

The Element of Air

When John ascended, I felt the cruel wanting from the memories my body holds of the intimacy we experienced, the nurturing love between Self and him. I felt this inner cradling and yet was seemingly all alone in this mournful wanting. I had not yet known that it was The Divine that held me close, cradling and singing the same lullabies to me that I sang to my son while he was yet in my womb and after his birth. I was not alone, for my Soul, seated in the throne of my heart, was closely connected with The Divine, even when I thought I had been abandoned by Them in my desolation.

Recall earlier my sense of being crushed by the lava flow and finding myself in the fetal position of a Lava Egg. Oddly enough, a scene from the last episode of *The Vikings* provided me with a visual that was resonant of how I was feeling at the time. It very accurately depicts the death all parents of ascended children experience, and the one-step, one-breath process of emergence we seek to find. Allow all your senses to become activated within the unfolding of the story...

A mother's child was stolen from her by an intruder, who later took the child's life. It was only after the intruder was executed by the Viking leader, and justice was achieved, that the mother entered fully into her mourning. She retreated into herself to find Self again. She welcomed the lonely solitude in which she would need to sit in the boughs of her living Hell and befriend this inner darkness, reconciling to the fact that it would be forever her reality. Like a tomato worm enters into a cocoon, transforming into the larvae that emerges into a hummingbird moth, she stepped from this world into the lava egg as her own cocoon.

Her internal landscape was a mirror of the external landscape – one created by the eruption of the volcano lava that had spewed and scorched the life that had once existed many years before her. Her egg formed from a mixture of the desolate, black lava ash, fallen branches, dead leaves of the trees, and honey. The bitter smell of decaying, dried twigs and leaves mimicked her own bitter death that she was forced to endure. The honey, the sweet memories of a life well-lived with her son, continued to nourish her in her desinence.

Several items belonging to her son and a water skin were placed within the bowl of her lava egg. As she entered into the hollow nest of the egg, she felt her own vulnerable hollowness consume her. She covered herself in her bareness, having entered into the world with nothing and departing from the world, from who she was, with nothing. As she curled up like a new babe in her mother's womb, the same mixture was spread upon her body, encasing her in her capsule of living-death. Several blankets of furs were placed upon her and the top of her egg, encapsulating her in her darkness that was in solidarity with her scorched, shredded existence. She and her egg were then sealed with the honey and earthen mixture. Tiny holes perforated her lava egg, offering her the breath she felt she couldn't take in her living-death. The egg was a ceremonial, symbolic state of grace for her as she commenced her journey. She had entered the abyss of her living-death. She would emerge from the darkness, where she dwelled in the recesses of a shattered heart, to be reborn into an as-yet-unknown being.

The moment I witnessed this form of ceremonial process for a parent whose child had ascended I desired this same ceremonial process for myself. How I longed to have had this loving ceremony afforded to me so I might have known, in that moment, what only later occurred to me: that I had also died. I had become the egg and within the egg, life dwelled. Within my living-death, there was life.

In the *Book of Mary of Magdalene*, one of the "lost" books of Jesus' teachings, Mary is called to speak to officials in Caesar's government on those teachings. At one point she picked up an egg and compared it to the human Soul. Referring to Jesus' ascension, she proclaimed that just as an egg holds life within the life before the life emerges, so the Soul re-emerges and returns to life. The leaders jokingly remarked that there was as great a chance of that as the egg she held turning red. In that moment, the egg miraculously turned red. In our death, awaiting our rebirth in our own lava egg, our Soul Season plants a seed that requires germination. That germination is the revelation that within our child's life existed a life of pure love, and in their death there is new life. For in our life existed their life, and in our living-death their life still exists, for within our living-death there is new life fulfilled by love. Within the lava egg is our life, waiting to birth life, for life, in and from pure love. Our heart weeps because we aren't aware, in our humanness, that this pure love is who we are at our core – our Soul. Our lava egg holds us in this love, which is stronger than death.

In her 2019 book, *Mary Magdalene Revealed: The First Apostle, Her Feminist Gospel & the Christianity We Haven't Tried Yet*, Meggan Watterson shares her take on the passage where Mary was found weeping at the tomb of Jesus, by Jesus (whom she thinks is the caretaker of the tomb) and two angels. They ask her, "Why are you weeping?" Mary weeps because of her love for Jesus, a love stronger than death. Meggan adds this, which is a powerful insight for all parents of ascended children:

…"A love that is a power we have always been worthy of. A love that is a power with us, from within us. A love that brings us back to life, again and again."

Jesus asks us why we are weeping and desires us to know that we are worthy of a love beyond death. That love resides within our living-death, our emergence, and our rebirth found within each of the seasons and their transitional phases. The love that exists between our Self and our child is the *love that brings us back to life, again and again.* I offer this poem to reflect upon during this season of the Soul.

Self Portrait
It doesn't interest me if there is one God
Or many gods.
I want to know if you belong or feel
Abandoned.
If you know despair or can see it in others.
I want to know

If you are prepared to live in the world
With its harsh need
To change you. If you can look back
With firm eyes
Saying this is where I stand. I want to know
If you know
How to melt into that fierce heat of living
Falling toward
The center of our longing. I want to know
If you are willing
To live, day by day, with the consequence of love
And the bitter
unwanted passion of your sure defeat.

I have heard, in that fierce embrace,
Even the Gods speak to God.

— David Whyte

EXPERIENTIAL ACTIVITIES
TO AID IN THE SEASON OF THE SOUL'S
SEED OF REBIRTH

1. **Journaling/Writing**: Journaling is just another word for writing what is in our inner landscape in the moment. As I write this memoir for my Self and all of you, I write from the inner landscapes I have experienced and am experiencing while I write. Science has overwhelmingly shown us how writing stimulates and engages numerous sensory and motor cortical regions of the brain, and is now finding this to be so in the neurological centrum of the heart as well. In the process, it synthesizes the internal and external landscapes. Writing is also a spiritual ritual that tethers the Soul to Spirit, removing the veil that seemingly separates one from their loved one. Journaling is a prayer that offers one a space to share, fully, what is in one's heart and mind. It extends an invitation to a parent of an ascended child to scream into the abyss of their grief. In the original Hebrew text, the Bible tells us that because God gave us the Word, the words humans speak and think are sacred. As we think, we write, and as we write, we speak to God/Spirit. This is the mysticism of writing. As we write in our journals, we are given the gift of a direct connection with God/Spirit. With this connection we are given permission to release and receive with a Divine love that brings us back to life again and again.

2. **Participate in a Spiritual Wilderness Quest/Retreat**: Taking a walk in the natural elements of the Earth brings one closer to The Divine, for the Earth was created before humankind to aid us in all our needs. As the seasons offer us insight and guidance about where we are psychologically in our grief journey and our daily life moving forward, so does the external landscape offer us the gift of divine touch. There are several offerings to assist one in their spiritual quest:

    a. **Local Solo Wilderness Quest**: Go on a solo wilderness quest from dawn to dusk at a local national/city/state park. Inform at least one person of your destination and take a form of communication in case of emergency, which is turned off otherwise. The point of the wilderness quest is to reach inside your Soul's tether to Spirit so you can touch the face of your child within The Divine. This is a spiritual journey where the individual seeks to be closer to one's purest self, the higher Self. The greater-than-human world is a safe space to allow one to seek without shame, guilt, resentment, and judgment. On my website at https://cynthiaeyer.kartra.com/page/home I have created a page to assist one in how to prepare and journey on a solo wilderness quest.

b. **Shaman-Led Vision Quest:** This type of quest is led by a spiritual healer and can last an evening, as in a sweat lodge setting, or up to four days, as in the wilderness vision quest I attended. One can find a local offering with a simple Google search. I hope to lead one someday, so stay tuned. The best way I can explain a shaman-led vision quest is by sharing my own experience of my place in the wilderness and the psychological and spiritual support Divine offered me there.

On the morning of the first of four days of our Vision Quest, I rose before Grandfather Sun had gifted us with light. I lay in my hammock and listened to the silence, as if awaiting Their guidance for me before I ventured out into the wilderness. I untied and rolled up my hammock and put my gear together, readying myself for the trek to the chosen spot, then joined the others for morning tea. I wondered how hungry I would get and whether that human physical need would interrupt my spiritual connection, as hunger reverberates in our mind.

We gathered in silence and one by one crossed the threshold of the entrance from our community camp to the wilderness we each would take to journey to our chosen spots. The threshold held its own Divine magic, palpable as I neared it and crossed through it to the other side. It was as if God was telling me, Their daughter, that all had been prepared for me in Their kingdom and I would be granted passage into the kingdom during the solitary quest. The spot The Divine chose for me reminded me of a mystical place in the lands of the Fae. In the early, wee morning hours I would be greeted with a fine mist that rose from the small stream beside the circle of birch trees where my hammock was strung. An iridescent green moss grew all around me and a pair of hummingbirds nested close by.

As a psychology major, I sought the psychology within the spiritual experiences and the spiritual within the psychological experiences. I opened my mind to the awe and wonder instead of the mundane. I hadn't drawn since my son's ascension and as I opened my mind the need to draw from that place of awe came through and filled my days. I journaled, and yet the words couldn't express the truth I experienced as much as the drawing did. During one such time, as I sat on a fallen tree and drew what God was sharing with me in the scene, the female hummingbird started touching her beak to the peach-colored buttons on my shirt, flitting about me, perching on my head, landing on the back collar, touching down next to my elbow, beak once again attempting to drink the nectar she assumed would come from the button. Perhaps she was just offering me a warm welcome into the kingdom. Every day after that first day, she and her partner would be there in the morning with their song, offering me their gratitude for accepting the invitation to their home.

I walked in the creek bed, I bathed in the fresh water coming down from the top of the Colorado mountains. The trees offered me their support and shelter during my stay in their forest. One of the trees in the circle was supported between two other trees, and I thought that if a stronger wind came by it would topple on me. This is where I learned to let go of the mundane and trust God and the place they offered me in the world after emerging from Their kingdom. I don't trust well, and God was asking me to trust Them, that They already have plans for me.

c. **Attend a Healing Circle:** Healing Circles are also known as Talking or Counsel Circles and utilize a "talking piece" to serve as the "amplifier" for what is inside of one that seeks the healing the circle offers. The Healing Circle is symbolic of the cycle of life, the eternity of life, death, and rebirth, by which all life is interrelated and interconnected. The Healing Circle goes beyond the veil to Spirit. Elders, teachers, and psychotherapists use the Healing/Talking Circle as a place to teach important lessons about the sanctity of all of life and Spirit's place in life. Unity churches have resources to assist one in finding a Healing Circle in their local area. The Unity Church I attend has a monthly Healing Circle for all to attend. Jesus taught His disciples in a circle and within that circle all received healing through discussion. This is the essence of a healing circle.

3. **The Rhythm of the Universe**: As above, so below. Before there were words from God, there was sound, for sounds combined in a format for all to communicate are known as words. Allow the rhythm of music, dance, painting, drawing, singing, writing, et cetera to move in and through you with unabashed surrender: The Seeding Season listens to the rhythmic dance of the energies of the Universe, the essence of their creative self, emerging into the fullness of life in Summer. The fields of science and psychology have shown that these forms of creativity are expressions of what exists within and demands release. In the early, wee hours of the morning I sometimes sit with tea and offer gratitude within the sounds of song to The Divine. I close my eyes and just allow what wants to emerge from me to be set free. It always releases with a mix of sorrow and joy, my tears the cleansing healing of my Soul, heart, and mind. The release opens me so that I may receive the love that offers me the gift of life again. My two kitties are always close, if not on my lap and by my side offering their connection to my existence in that moment. This is a form of meditation that offers us the stillness by which we enter the realm of Spirit and receive their loving healing again and again.

4. **Meditation**: There are many forms of meditation. I am a Deepak Chopra-certified Primordial Sound Meditation Instructor and will be

creating an advanced meditation program in the near future. Here is a list of some basic forms of meditation which can be practiced alone or in a group. The energy of a group aids in a consistent practice.

a. I practice sound meditation, followed by silence for a period of time, usually 15 to 30 minutes. The sound is my voice, but sound can be drums, singing bowls, bells, chimes, et cetera.

b. I practice walking meditations. I go out to hiking trails and take a walk-about in the forest in silence. The openness of the forest and sky above us removes the sense of confinement that may exist in one's internal landscape. Spirit resides in all creation and all creation is a conduit for Spirit. I like walking with at least one other person when I practice walking meditations in forests. It feels both comforting and safe.

c. There are several specific breathing meditations. Breathing meditations are a very powerful form of mindfulness where one focuses only on their breath. One's breath has its own innate rhythm and flow in the inhale and exhale. Once one enters into the innate rhythm and flow of breath, this same rhythm and flow synchronizes with all that is experienced in life. The heart and mind become one, releasing the ego of attachment, allowing for peace beyond understanding.

SEASON OF THE BODY BETWEEN EMERGENCE AND REBIRTH

*"And He said: 'I tell you the truth, **unless you change and become like little children, you will never enter the kingdom of heaven.** Therefore, whoever humbles himself like this child is the greatest in the kingdom of heaven. And whoever welcomes a little child like this in My name welcomes Me.*

—Matthew 18:3-5 (NIV)

Season of Emergence Represents:

Season of Summer

The Child

The Body

The ID

Innocence

Birth and Rebirth

Spirit in Water

Direction of South

Eros of Self-Love

In our rebirth, we are the child teaching the adult how to care for them. Do you remember when your first child was born and you learned to take your cues for his/her care from them? Our child season is teaching us how to care for ourselves in our rebirth. We are like the "little children" that Jesus talks about in Matthew 18:3-5, seeking love, attention, care, and guidance from The Divine for evolving into who we now are. We humble ourselves and learn to get our heart, mind, body, and soul on the level of our babe. The child doesn't hold onto the last moment, for only the current moment exists and what lies ahead. The emergence asks us to let go of what was and to seek what is to be.

The body informs us of what is needed, physically, in the season of the child. We bump into life all over again, learning what it is like to be reborn into the great world, which is quite humbling all on its own. Not only is this season humbling, it helps us to acquire our truth in what and who is needed in our rebirth. We journey into a deep appreciation of the strength that exists within our vulnerability as a person. We see with new eyes and ears, as we remember our very life with our child and Spirit. We begin to understand the depths of Jesus' love as He reminds us in Mark 8:18: *"Do you have eyes but fail to see, and ears but fail to hear? And don't you remember?"* (NIV).

We begin to remember our whole self, and start to re-member our heart, mind, and body to our Soul as one being with Spirit in our rebirth. Our Soul remembers that it shares its very memory as the lifeblood with the tiny little babe we emerge into. We learn patience we thought we never had. We remember what it is like to not have a voice to relate what we need and desire, thus offering the babe within unconditional, empathetic, compassionate love. We *"see"* for the first time with new eyes that go beyond the physical, deep into the very Soul and heart of the child we each emerge into. We begin to really listen to what is not being communicated more than what is. We begin to recognize each of the elements within the season of the child within our own emergence back into an honored-life, for each element is the essence of who we are, our truth of where we are while traveling within and through the seasons. I offer you the elements that are the essence of us as a child.

The Season of Summer symbolizes the birth of all that did not exist prior. The bare branches have survived the cold, bitter winds of dark storms of our inner landscapes, requiring that we go deep within to retrieve our internal light. The planted seed of hope then emerges through the warm spring rains of our Soul, lifting to the rays of hope we had been seeking. This emergence is not without struggle, for it is in the struggle we are the most vulnerable; however, we find within the courage to withstand the energy and to crack our lava-shelled egg and cast light upon our darkness.

The Element of Water symbolizes the womb's living waters that flow within us. Living waters quench the dry desert landscape that has stolen the life from us. The quenching waters turn into a rain that drops life upon us – they are the gift offered us from our Soul still in union with Spirit. The rains shower us with a love that lives beyond death. It is the promise of new life which now floods us, readying us for our re-birth and pushing us through our emergence.

The Direction of South symbolizes the nautical direction that signals we are going in a flow of living waters, and informs us where we go when we want to play outside. We go to the water's edge to our favorite lake, stream, and beach, running and splashing into its depths like little children released from the confines to play with abandon. We re-member our entire being surrendered to the joy of the sounds of laughter, boundless energy, and smells of freshness and promise as the body frees itself of isolation and darkness. We taste the sense of life as juicy fullness, like eating ripe juicy melons and oranges, dripping down our chins, and laughter in the air knowing that this is the season of living without reservation.

The Wide-Eyed Innocence symbolizes seeing the world with awe and wonder, not yet knowing what fear feels like in the body, for the mind is not yet fully aware. The new fawn lives life from internal senses of pure survival, learning that life is full of surprises that reach out and bump into it. In this way it is experiencing life for what it is, without expectations or knowing its own perceptive boundaries.

Birth/Re-Birth symbolizes how our physical, psychological, and spiritual being forms and changes during the processes of our cycle from living-death to honored-life. What is cultivated within is manifested outwardly. As we begin to emerge and shift our inner landscapes, our appearance begins to change from dry, sallow, and hollowed to bright and healthy. We are like the winter tree that had buds of promise in the Spring and now slowly, purposefully, reaches for the rays of light to nourish itself within the unfurling leaves. Some may seek to be baptized in a religious or spiritual sacrament using water. The essence of this emergence from our living-death to honored-life is a deeper understanding, a Divine gnosis of that sacrament, which I know to be of greater spiritual intensity than any other ritual we could ever be offered. In this birth we sense our spiritual awakening with every fiber, sinew, and bone in the essence of who we are as a result of walking the path of our living-death.

The ID is the psychological phase that seeks all experiences to be about the child him/herself. The "ID" is when the child learns to identify who they are in relation to the world and those in their immediate vicinity. The child learns who they can trust and not trust without inhibitions. This is the essence of the season that helps us recognize who has our permission to stay and who must be released. It is the ego personified who desires to experience life to its fullest with abandonment. This is how every child learns to play in life and not take life always in a state of seriousness. Even as fully developed adults, we must all periodically return to the season of the child so we don't forget what it is like, and so we can touch our child where he/she is. We must re-member.

The Body is an attunement tool by which we connect with Self, Spirit, each other, and our environment. Touch is how the child perceives the world around them and their experiences of the world. For an infant, and through childhood, touch occurs in all seven sensory centers. The child, as a novice experiencer, does not yet have a perception of attunement. Personal boundaries are not yet realized, thus leaving the child vulnerable and dependent upon his/her surroundings. This dependency is a sense of the world bumping into them and can be filled with both lightness and darkness. This form of lightness and darkness is one's humanity blooming. In falling down, the child wonders, in both fear and awe, how it occurred. It is one's reaction to the child when they fall that shapes the child's perception. If a parent, laughing and with wide-eyed inquisitiveness, asks the child what occurred when they fell, the child will mirror that reaction. This becomes their learned perception for every fall thereafter – mentally, physically, and psychologically – for in the darkness there is always light, and in what appears to be full of goodness lurks a point of darkness. It is the way of a human and it is the combination of one's light and dark aspects that we sit with and befriend. We are both the parent and the child for our human self and our spiritual Self in the season of emergence.

Sometimes the child in us remains quiet and illusive, desiring to take in the new sounds, sights, tastes, touches, smells, and feelings of their seven sensory perceptions from a distance. There is an offering around the sensory perceptions in the experiential activities of this section one can participate in to assist them in connecting with their body. Because the season of emergence centers around the sensory perception of touch, one may become the opposite of how they reached out prior to their living-death. Where one had been more touchy-feely with others, they may withdraw, and vice versa. It's important not to judge oneself or others. It's part of one's *re-membering* in their emergence. The world bumps into the child and the child learns to be perceptive of personal needs and desires in the experiences of the bumping.

Narcissistic Love as the ID is the quintessential child. The world bumping into the child teaches the child what feels good, not so good, and what will not be tolerated. As the child perceives being bumped and learns what he/she wants and needs, it is only natural to become narcissistic. The DSM V (book of psychological disorders/conditions) categorizes narcissism as a personality disorder, defining it as "a mental condition in which people have an inflated sense of their own importance, a deep need for excessive attention and admiration, troubled relationships, and a lack of empathy for others." I think narcissism gets a bad reputation because it is always discussed and defined as a social disorder in the DSM. I understand narcissism to be a Divine quality and that as long as that quality serves the greater good, it is a benefactor of Divine love. Look around you at the beautiful sculptures and architecture that have been built, like gothic churches, the Sistine Chapel, the Sydney Opera House, the Trevi Fountain in Rome, the Statue of Liberty, and the Joan of Arc Memorial. These are works of greatness: the worth of the artist in seeking a love for the greater good of all, realized from the creativity of the Soul connected with Spirit. Narcissism also abounds in non-human creation, where The Divine delights in the blooming fields of tulips, the awe and wonder of the bumble bee, the flight of the monarchs, the song of birds and their array of alluring plumage of mating dances, the inspirational and exquisite sunrises and sunsets. All of creation is narcissistic, and justifiably so. We are all majestic creations of awe and wonder, given the breath of life from living waters in love, from love, for love, with love from a Spiritual passion to love.

We are taught by various governing systems that we are not worthy and that we must earn our due both in life and death. We have forgotten. We have forgotten that we are created and birthed from love in love, an Agape love. We have lost our way to Spirit and must find our way back by way of the child. The season of the child helps us to remember Agape love and to re-member ourselves to Spirit within all creation. When we re-member, we return to our child-like wonder and enter the veil to visit with our child through our Self – our Soul in harmony with the rhythm of Divine love, bringing us back to life again and again.

EXPERIENTIAL ACTIVITIES
TO AIDE IN THE SEASON OF EMERGENCE
AS WE EXPAND FROM OUR REBIRTH

1. **Ceremonial Baptism** – Water ceremonies date back to the Mesopo-
tamian periods, and India has preserved their practices with water
as a sacred element of life for more than 4,500 years. Pagan rituals
with water as a sacred element for purification and rebirth date back
more than 3,700 years, before the Bronze Age. Christian ceremonies with water were considered pagan until around 1,200 AD but
are now widely used for new birth rituals and Baptism (a rebirth of
the Soul with Christ). Whatever your practice, choose what you feel
comfortable with and with whom you feel comfortable. The more
privately public (a public statement made in an intimate setting)
your ceremonial ritual, the more real it will be to you in terms of
your emergence.

Such ceremonies can take place in a bathtub, a lake, a river, a stream, a
church, a pool, et cetera. It can be in a circle created to symbolize your
eternal being through the seasons of your journey and your life. You
can choose full submersion, or water poured over your head or other
parts of your body. Wear whatever you want to wear or nothing at
all. Add whatever elements you wish, be it crystals, sages, herbs, flow-
ers, incense, et cetera. This is your ceremony. Create what "feels" true
to you. Journal your experience. Did you feel the water within you
flow with the same rhythm of your submersion? How did you "feel"
the water, externally and internally? What is your relationship with
the element of water now after the ritual exercise? Is it different from
what you felt and thought about water before you were submerged? If
you were previously baptized, how is being baptized from your living-
death different?

If you wish to share in the group what your ritual was and what you
experienced, we would love to hear from you.

2. **Wading in Water**: Go to a body of water and wade in the water for no less than 10 minutes. Come back to the spot two more times within a week's time. One may go to the same source of water, yet they will not experience the same water. Remember this as you journal your experiences and how that experience changed with each time. Did you feel the water within you flow with the same rhythm? How did you "feel" the water, externally and internally? What is your relationship with the element of water now after the wading experience? What arose in you before, during, and/or after wading? Did you choose to go deeper into the water and, if so, why? If you wish to share in the group what your ritual was, how you performed your ritual, and what you experienced, we would love to hear from you.

SEASON OF AWARENESS
BETWEEN
REBIRTH AND HONORED-LIFE

The Season of Awareness symbolizes:

Awareness of Emergence

Psychological/Mental/Emotional States from Memory

The Mind in Grief

The Adolescent

The Rule of Fear in Change

The Season of Fall

The Direction of West

The Element of Fire

The Gifts of the Dreamer

The Ego

The Eros of Self Love

The Season of Awareness is all about one's psychological and emotional state of being. After the emergence out of the darkness, when we're just learning how to be in the world again, this stage can be very agitating and rebellious. The mind begins to bump the world back, and we find our place in the world and how the world fits into that place. This season is both a liminal space and a human growth space. The awe and wonder from our emergence shift into rationalization, relativity, and relatability. Instead of wondering, one wanders toward the unknown. The wandering can feel confusing and disorientating. One begins to think they are "lost" and out of touch with reality and everyone else. Life may appear to be drifting in and out of focus, the fog of grief shifting, requiring one to seek clarity and meaning.

There are different forms that our immersions and emergences into and through the seasons take, and sometimes the forms take place simultaneously. Sometimes one experiences the seasons of emergence and awakening concurrently. In July 2006, I experienced such an emergence that awakened me to begin my inner quest for purpose. For three years after John's ascension, I had recurring dreams (nightmares) in which I was frantically attempting to see and speak with him, only to just miss him either because of his Naval mission or my Army mission. Each dream was born of my desperate need to reconnect and interact with my son again, to "see" him alive, hear his voice, and feel his vitality for life in my blood. I now see "mission" as a form of vision quest. Please allow me to explain in my telling of my "dream quest" that brought me to a simultaneous immersive awakening.

I was dreaming and I knew I was dreaming. I was the watcher watching the dreamer dream. The searching for and missing each other for the last three years ended with my son coming home, on military leave, for two weeks. At the end of our time together he was packing his bags and I was unrolling his clothes and putting them back into the drawers. Our conversations were being communicated telepathically. He told me to stop, that he had to go. I told him I didn't want him to go. Then I knew he knew he was not alive, that it was his Spirit visiting with me. I asked him who told him he was dead, and he told me he always knew. That he came to visit me in my dreams because I couldn't let him go. "Mom, please," he said, "I need to go, and I need you to let me go. I have another mission I need to go on." I could understand the depth of importance of his "mission," yet didn't know what it was. I told him okay, and that I loved him so very much and I missed him more deeply than I could convey. He told me how much he loved me and that he would see me again.

As mentioned earlier, on 21 September 2003, the day of John's ascension, he and two other warriors, Marc Lee and Brian Bill, were riding motorcycles together. The three were linked by the service of the B.U.D.S. and Navy SEALS programs, and Brian Bill was the Navy SEAL who was training and testing John and Marc to enter these programs. It was late July 2006, when John visited to tell me I needed to let him go because he had another mission. On August 2, 2006, Marc Lee ascended, becoming the first Navy SEAL to die in Iraq. That was John's "mission." Marc had protected his SEAL brothers from the enemy, and now John needed to meet him and walk him into the halls of Valhalla, the majestic hall for all warriors who die in the battle for the greater good. Some call this hall Heaven, yet I know there is a special place for warriors who make the ultimate sacrifice – their human life. Brian Bill would ascend on the battlefield, nearly to the day five years later, on 6 August 2011. I know he too was met by his SEAL brothers who had fallen before him, with Marc and John walking him into the halls of Valhalla. I also know that together, these warriors of Valhalla lead us all to fight the spiritual battle that brings us all back to remember and re-member our human selves in Divine relationship with Spirit.

One's search for clarity and meaning is one's awareness of who they are becoming, requiring answers to questions they didn't know existed within them – for them. Sometimes one finds themselves preferring the perpetual darkness this liminal space holds – the interminable hallway of the in-between, of two closed doors. In this space, their physical, emotional, mental, and spiritual being is questioned. It is in the questioning that we are offered clarity, hope, and the strength to transition into the next season, emerging from the perpetual darkness that can be confusing, and sometimes feel safe, found in the in-between. In the pursuit of clarity of one's inner landscape, one must reach for the handle of the next door or risk becoming eternally lost in the mind of grief, devoid of love, hope, and purpose. It is only through the next door that they will be able to step into an honored-life for self and their ascended child, with its infinite possibilities. We pass through the adolescence of our new life and return to the heart. The heart that holds the infinite love that allows us, beckons us, to live again and again.

Adolescent Mind: The adolescent mind reigns in this season, wanting what it wants because it thinks it is what is best for them. Awareness is about coming out of the body and paying more attention to the mind, the ego in motion, which gives us our emotions about life and how life fits into us. The season of awareness can feel overwhelming – tiring and withering us. Sometimes I visualize a desert as my inner landscape when I find myself in this season. I procrastinate because I feel in my body and my mind a grave lack of energy. I desire what was and grieve what is, all the while knowing that this liminal space is where I currently reside.

Other times I see my inner landscape as a forest on fire with the most vibrant, alluring colors that The Divine could ever paint our world with. The colors saturate my mind with a desire to just stay where I am. I want this and only this. I want the beauty and vivaciousness it offers, reminding me of the motto John lived by: "You can sleep when you're dead, Mom, life is to be lived now!" Yet Fall is also a season that reminds us the fun times will soon be over, with the juices of fresh fruits flowing no more. This season can be both frustratingly confusing and delightfully alluring because it is both a liminal space and a human growth season.

When our emergence from the darkness of Winter and Spring results in an almost immediate re-immersion into humanity, and we are in the awareness stage of our emergence, that immersion is not always kind. I remember such a re-immersion after completing the wilderness vision quest I attended during my master's program. My acute awareness had come back into play, and my return to the world felt like an assault on all my sensory centers. I just wanted to go back into the darkness. It felt safe there, for in the darkness I could openly grieve and not have to meet the expectations of systems and people. At the same time I wanted, and needed, to emerge from the darkness and step out into the world, learning in both mind and body how to be again. My body and heart wanted to stay in the darkness and my mind rebelled. I didn't want to talk, and I talk a lot. I couldn't find the words to communicate all that had awakened, and was still awakening, in me. What words I could say didn't give the experience any justice. Silence, I realized, was the best way I could honor what The Divine had given me in my four days of solitude during the vision quest.

In fact, the silence I experienced in the wilderness during those four days without food or other modern amenities offered me a sense of great solace and brought me back to The Divine. My mind had been rebelling against Them, still feeling abandoned by Them because of John's ascension. Before the quest, Dr. Tina Fields, the professor for the wilderness quest, told me she could visibly see how I questioned my faith in Christ, seeking the answers I so desperately needed to bring me back to Them, The Divine. After the Quest, she said she saw that I had *re-membered* myself to Them and that this was one of the most profound transformations she had witnessed in her years of teaching Ecopsychology.

The Season of Fall helps us to come face to face with that which must be released. Even when that thing has an appearance of being healthy, it doesn't necessarily mean that it is healthy for us. Chlorophyll, which is created in the stems and leaves of trees, floral, and fauna, is the food that gives them their energy. In the Fall, the trees and plants shed their need to hold chlorophyll in their stems and leaves. Their innate sense of well-being knows that doing so would cause the very thing that keeps them vibrant to wither them. They must release the chlorophyll so that in the season of winter their leaves and stems won't freeze and take what energy is needed to emerge in the late Spring and fully bloom in the Summer. Releasing the chlorophysll is also what aides the leaves in turning the vibrant, fiery tones that colors our Fall landscapes so vividly. Even those leaves and stems that still hold some green must be released to offer the trees and plants a time of restoration.

Fall is the season and liminal space between the fullness of life and wealth of abundance present in Summer, to the stillness and absence of abundance coming forth in Winter. It is also the season that offers mindfulness and thought to our desires and needs, not only governing intention with purpose for ourselves but glimpsing the heart for community in our choices. There are still some juicy bits of life left, and Fall asks us to offer gratitude in the changes that take place when we no longer hold onto that which does not serve us in the moment. One only needs to look at the vibrancy of Fall's colors, as if the very forest is on fire, to offer gratitude for what was, is, and will become. Fall offers us a reflection of what release looks like, smells like, tastes like, sounds like, and feels like as we walk through the forest of our rebirth and life yet to come.

The facets of release are a testament to what room the release offers us in the next season. This release showed up in my dream state when I visited with John. I was abundantly grateful, having already experienced the fullness of him and then the sudden negation of him in my human life. Mentally, I released the need to keep searching for him. Psychologically, I released my need to repeat the fears that existed in my body, that rule of fear that overwhelms us because our entire being has changed from what was to the unknown. When that fear came to me as he said he needed to leave, I had only to open my heart with gratitude and remember. Physically, it was the memory of the tragic event of John's ascension, which my body was continuing to experience through the dreams and panic attacks, that I released. Spiritually, I released my control, steeped in the well of fear. I had to come to a place of faith. Faith in God and Goddess having my son. I had to remember and re-member who I am now without my son, yet whole in mind, body, and Soul with Spirit. Fall is the fire, the light of understanding, as I came full circle from my living-death into the birth of an honored-life.

One will go through the seasons again, and again, as they transition into a greater, deeper understanding and awareness of who they are without their child. As I came full circle in my own seasonal transitions, I found my life was transitioning into a new life without my son within it. Even though there were times when I still found myself back in my darkness, not yet knowing how to proceed, I knew I was seeking a way to rebirth the purpose of my life to honor my life without my son, in honor of him. I had to go full circle a few more times until I was able to take my pain, sorrow, and hope and transform it into a gift of love. A gift of love that not only offers me the gift of life again and again, it offers all whose child has ascended, and those who support them, a gift of love that leads them back to life, again and again. In this gift I offer I also offer myself and my son an honorable life within the gift.

The Eros of Self-Love is borne of one's willingness to be sharpened by the **Fires of Divine Love** and into the truth of Self-Love. I like to say it is the eros of "selfish" love. Self-Love, tested by the fires that parents of ascended children emerge from, is learned through little experiences that hold profound messages that offer us gratitude through resting in Divine Love. Something very profound came out of that dream visit with John. The last thing I prayed before John's accident was for him to always be held in the safety of The Divine. That They protect him. They helped me to realize that it isn't our bodies that They protect, it's our Souls. Our Souls live on forever, and so They keep "Us" safe from the fear of the darkness. They are the small pin light that shines in our darkness when we decide to befriend the darkness and seek the meaning it holds for us so that we can offer ourselves and others the light. The Divine is our armor. They are what John, and Marc, and Brian put on before going on their missions. John still comes to visit me on occasion. He appears to others to leave messages for me and I feel him at times when my heart is open to receive Spirit. Our bond, as a single mom and her only child, is a love so deep, wide, and entrusting, that not even death can separate us. It is the sacredness of our love, intwined with my life, that brings me back to life again and again.

PSYCHOLOGY
OF THE SEASONS

*"People will do anything, no matter how absurd, to avoid facing
their own souls."*
*"One does not become enlightened by imagining figures of light,
but by making the darkness conscious."*

—Carl G. Jung

Today I wake up in the space that exists between my Seasons; in the
deep sleep of nothingness and the wake that crushes me in the deep
recesses of my heart. I wake in the Child Season, the birth of a new dawn.
Inside I am crying and kicking, and screaming, like a child not wanting
to leave her slumber and face the bully on the playground. I see myself
in my mind's eye standing with my fists at my side, stomping my foot at
the Divine. I tell Them with much anger and pain that I don't want to be
responsible and face one more day without my son. They see my pain.
Deep down, I want Them to save me without my participation – and I
also know my participation is necessary. In other words, I have to be willing to put on my boots and pull myself up by the bootstraps.

I lay here, having a conversation with Them without words. Words aren't necessary, for They know my heart. Besides, words can't possibly convey what my heart feels. I lay here, in the still, dark wee hours of the morning, the darkness a reminder of the season in which my heart and mind are currently residing. I lie still and listen…and breathe. My two-year-old, still a kitten at heart who has no notion of what boundaries are, curls up at my head, her paws on my face. Her purring, a loud message of Divine love. My six-year-old cat lies in wait for me to extend my hand and stroke her. These two are instruments of The Divine, from The Divine, of Their love and how they care for me in my journey. I breathe in that love in gratitude and ask The Divine how to proceed. *One step, one breath, one moment at a time,* They tell me. This is the armor the Word tells us is Them.

The world tells us that armor is an outward sign of the strength that exists within. The Soul shows us that Their armor is an outward sign of our vulnerability requiring protection. I am not strong like everyone thinks I am. I am weak and vulnerable and it is only when I allow my Soul to take the lead and will my mind and heart to just breathe, that I am capable of facing the day one step, one moment, one breath at a time. I breathe in Their love – the pause, a moment of gratitude – and breathe out that loving gratitude.

This experience is written out in my journal, and I am guided to share it to show how the simple acts of waking and readying myself for the life that is waiting in the moments before me is a seasonal transition come full circle. Sometimes that circle takes a few hours; other times, it takes days, weeks, months, or years. The amount of time isn't what is important, but one's willingness to give themselves permission to take one step, one moment, one breath after the other. It is the gift one offers themselves, as is the willingness to participate in the dynamics that offer them loving and kind support. Sometimes humans can be too much in their head and not willing to just let Spirit flow through. The very act of picking up the pen and putting oneself to paper holds the gift of movement and flow in harmony with The Divine. In seeing the writing, one sees "I." Hope lies within. In seeing oneself in the writing they find they have helped their Self cope with the darkness and sense the shift. The Soul plants a seed and asks The Divine to care for it while the human puts on the armor to take the first step, the first breath, of the moment.

The first step occurs in the season of emergence where life starts out a little wobbly. A cuppa and a moment of meditation turn to hope and the unlimited possibilities that lie before us. The experience in that moment turns to thoughts as the adolescent mind imagines each of those possibilities, the lists being ticked for accomplishment and how those accomplishments serve both the individual and the collective greater good. Pondering on forms of community, like work, school, yoga studio, church, doctor and/or shopping interactions elevate one from the mind to the heart. During these interactions one's very presence is shared. For us, parents of ascended children, that sharing is both our human self and higher Self, intertwined with the very essence of our child. When people begin to stop, look into the eyes of another, and truly "see" that person, people will begin to share with compassion on a collective level. What affects one affects all as we unknowingly and unwittingly share the energy that is who we are in that moment. How many times are you drawn to someone that has, unbeknownst to you and them, shared similar experiences, career paths, philosophies, skills, and/or hobbies? And, when you find you share similar experiences, you also find a sense of camaraderie of brotherhood and sisterhood?

In the moments of those experiences, because of our willingness to put on the armor and take one step, one moment, one breath in front of the other (even without verbalizing a request), The Divine sends us someone to care for us and us for them in our seasons and liminal spaces of need. One can never truly know what shoes one is wearing until one is willing to see them. Likewise, one can never truly understand what shoes we parents of ascended children are wearing until we are willing to *be seen*. Most therapy doesn't come from a licensed therapist in one-hour sessions. Healing, through learning *how* to cope, comes from within the deepest, darkest recesses of the heart and the willingness to have the heart to sit with one's darkness. My morning experience moving through the seasons is my willingness to have the heart to sit with my darkness. The heart shines the light of gratitude for the gifts the darkness harbors. We are the vessel that holds the weary state of our shattered humanity and the darkness is the safe harbor where our Soul resides, awaiting our return to life, again and again.

When we can look at our moments in this way, we are more capable of coping with how we traverse and travel our journey. We are alone inside. There is none other inside us but ourselves – our mind, heart and Soul are the only elements that exist within our human body. Seeing how the Seasons resonate in our consciousness of this, we can better visualize our journey and remove the fear of the darkness that we find ourselves steeped in.

Through the seasons and the awareness of Self in each of them, parents of ascended children are better capable of coping with the moments, breaths, and changes one experiences as they cycle through deaths and rebirths. Each death and rebirth of our journey is like a stepping stone across the rapids of the water of life. Some are close and easy to maneuver, and some require us to stretch and have faith in our Self, each other, and The Divine. Each step we take to the next stone is solely our choice. We are responsible for our willingness to participate. Even a "No" is a full sentence and a willing acceptance to participate. A No is an acceptance to participate on one's own terms and not be influenced to react on another's. An action is a mindful response, where a reaction is a mirrored response to re-act what is received. This is the choice all have, to be for themselves first and then for others. This is the awareness of Self one becomes when traversing their journey through the lens of the seasons.

The seasons of the inner landscapes of grief help us perceive our grief from different viewpoints, with lenses of different colors changing our perception. Some take the words perceive, viewpoint, and perception as interchangeable. They are not, though they do coincide. One's viewpoint is where one *is* in an experience, while one perceives with eyes wide open, with blinders on, or shut altogether – it is what one is willing to see. Perception is one's history thus far and how they choose to permit those experiences to color the lens through which they perceive life – again, with eyes open wide, shut tight, or with blinders to obscure. All live life with all three choices in play at different times of their life and within each experience. It's through the seasons we begin to recognize what lens we choose and why. It's through the mindful activity we take through the seasons that we are better capable of offering, first to ourselves and then each other, kindness and grace. This is the journey of being a Soul experiencing its humanness.

The lens one is willing to learn to see through is a direct reflection of the grace in their human experience. The Divine asks us to put on Their armor so that we may be in harmony *with* Them. So that They may be the rhythm of each step in each moment that we breathe. As we come into harmony with Their rhythm, we learn we are part of, not separate from, the "rhythm of the Universe" as Them. The rhythm of the Universe is witnessed and experienced in the outer landscapes and seasons of those landscapes. Divine rhythm elevates the grace of the seasonal landscapes as reflections of our inner landscapes. This lens is how one is capable of seeing beyond the veil, witnessing the mysteries of life that are being opened to them so that they may honor their child's life through them. This awareness beyond the veil brings us to a place with The Divine in Divine love. In the stepping out in the moments of life, Spirit creates within us a breath of love that offers new life from a place of love. The love found in stepping out and through the internal landscapes of our journey is the Divine love that brings us back to life, for Self and our child, again and again.

LIFE, RELATIONAL,
AND SPIRITUAL IMPACTS

I remember myself as a child, laying on the floor watching *Wild King-dom* and *Walt Disney World* on TV. I was so engrossed that I was completely unaware of anything or anyone else and cared not for the noise I heard. It was the same, beginning at age four, when I was sitting or lying on the floor reading Mother's *Children's Bible*. This Bible was huge, with lots of pictures to animate the stories for me. My favorite that continues to come back to me was "David and the Lion's Den."

In these two scenarios, parents of ascended children are David, or Souls experiencing what it is to be a human in grief and fear, and the lion is the dark, abysmal grief and persistent fear experienced by humans. Like the child, so engrossed in the scene that repeatedly unfolds in front of them, they aren't even aware of anything or anyone else. The show *Wild Kingdom* is the world the mind and heart live in, filled with danger, awe, and wonder. The landscapes and habitats are unknown to them except for what is inferred and informed. The lion stalks them in the darkness of who they now are in the living-death. Like the story of David and the Lion, the only savior is The Divine of one's faith, for to them all else has forsaken them.

It's hard for others to know this. They aren't experiencing what and who a parent of an ascended child is in that season of living-death. Others aren't living in the same experience of the initial shock and what follows for them. Until I wrote this book, I didn't know everything I was experiencing and thus could not even hope to explain. People who come to support these parents in whatever way(s) they know how to be for them may not understand. Their own expectations of how the parents are "supposed" to respond to them get in their way. It's not done maliciously. It just *is*. It is the innate human response steeped in a taught fear of what rejection *looks* like. Others don't realize that the parents aren't rejecting the offered support, but rather, their vision is tunneled by the dark abyss they find themselves in. They are capable only of seeing the permeance of the situation.

Parents go through motions they don't know they are going through. I still find myself talking without hearing myself. I still scream without sound, my tears are my heart flowing downstream, winding, shifting, banging against the shorelines and boulders of life I must engage in until I meet myself again in the great open sea of life. There is a saying that one can never walk in the same waters ever again, because those waters are in constant change, transitioning from one form, one place to another. Parents of ascended children will come to recognize themselves as those waters, and that who they were will not be who they are now or who they are to become. Relationships, careers, mindsets, and spiritual faiths will be tested, examined, redefined, reviewed, reshaped, and amended. There are stepping stones in our water as we cross the divide. When we get to a stepping stone, we rest before we continue our journey. I can't speak for others on how these areas affected them and were affected by their living-death and will affect them as they continue to transition into an honored-life. What I share may be similar to yours or someone you know. My prayer is that my experiences in these areas and the awareness given to me can help another.

RELATIONAL IMPACTS

Relationships are the most prevalent and visceral alterations all will experience. The human race, like other pack animals, innately seeks meaningful and safe relationships with each other. Parents of ascended children feel the impact of relationships more acutely than other people. Their living-death robs them of meaning and nothing feels safe. Their "home" has been shattered, burned, and covered over in the flow of lava that quickens to stifle their breath. They must traverse their journey, seemingly alone, to emerge into a new life that honors themselves so they can honor their child through them. There are many reasons for the beginning of some relationships and the ending of others along the journey. Both are okay, and it's important to remember one's own humanity in all decisions – even when a decision doesn't seem, or feel, like it was the right one.

When my family traveled to Virginia, they came out of deep love for both me and John. They came to support me in any way they could. I love them for that. At the same time, all I wanted was my son. His closest friends surrounded me, including Marc and Brian. John O'Hara was a roommate of John's and we still stay in very close contact with each other. It was those people who I stayed close to so I could "feel" my son's energies, alive in those close friends. My family didn't hold John's energy in them like John's close "brothers" and promised fiancé did – and do – however, when my son made friends, those friends became his family. That is our way. This connection is what I sought out in that crucial pivoting point of my life. I wasn't ignoring my family nor rejecting their care and love for me and John. I was lost in a very dark forest and his closest friends were the beacons of light, offering me glimpses of my son. (Even now, I prefer being around my brothers' children because they are close to the age John would have been. I live vicariously through them and their lives and the similarities of the ties my son would have lived with them and in them.) Back then, my family didn't understand that I was seeking out these "glimpses," and so their expectations were dashed against the crumbled stones of the relationship they had with him and me. Of course, John's friends and family were going through a similar "death" of a very intimate relationship; however, I'm not sure they understood the depth of what that meant for them, then and moving forward. Most see John as "gone," not realizing that he lives within each of them, as they each lived within John. I am thinking and hoping that will change when they read this.

Starting and Ending Relationships are both necessary to find, redefine, and regain one's grounding in a living-death to an honored-life. The grounding aids in redefining one's purpose, one's new definition of what a legacy is. I have come to understand, as a single parent of an only child who has ascended, that one's legacy comes from one's purpose. One's purpose, as a soul experiencing what it is to be a human, is to simply be love and receive love. We are born in the love, from the love of The Divine, and are not to forget that love is who we are as children of The Divine. I understand this as one of the meanings in Christ's teachings to *be in the world, not of the world.* How one goes about sharing that love and receiving that love is one's legacy.

There are many types of relationships that are compromised, lost, gained, renewed, and converted in impactful ways when one's child ascends. I do want to add that when one compromises, there is a winner and a loser. I encourage all to not compromise their integrity, honesty, and truth, regardless of how difficult the encounter, circumstances, or relationship is in that moment. In the beginning of my grief and sorrow, I did compromise my own truth when I gave up trying to see the deeper intentions of a friend when she used my son's love for me as an emotional tool against me. I know she didn't mean to use him this way, however, in her own grief she did. I gave up looking and seeing. I gave up hearing and listening. I gave up reason and understanding. I gave up on myself and who I was as a vessel for my son's integrity, honesty, and truth that now resides within me. I permitted another's interpretation of what I was saying to compromise my whole being. I could see what I needed to say in response and no longer cared. Her inquiry of me, paired with her statement of how my son saw me, felt incomprehensible.

My friend was like a sister to me and a second mom to John. I stood by her, for her, when her own family betrayed her. In that moment, I felt the full impact of all the betrayals she was feeling inside of her and couldn't help her. In that moment she took all that feeling and emotion and poured it on me. I felt like I was back in the lava egg, blinded, deafened, and dying. My friend was in so much pain and I think she needed me to not be in her life because I was a reminder of her pain and the secrets that pain carried.

In the moment I folded and compromised my own truth I lost her respect and trust in how she saw me, just as she had lost my respect and trust in how I saw her. The little girl who endured so much trauma in her childhood, learning to carry secrets as lies, came to the surface, took charge, lied, and then wanted to just run away. Just as a little girl, I didn't run away, I stayed and chose to be compliant. Fear had taken me. Fear of not being enough. Fear of the loss of one more person I loved deeply and totally. Fear in the perceived loss of what the world tells us is our legacy through our children. Fear of the darkness I re-entered. Fear of David's lion.

Time has passed and I see that interaction from both sides. I see that it was, and is, so much more than the question and answers posed. I see her in her own raw vulnerability in that time of her life and her sorrow and pain in my son's ascension. In retrospect, her need to end our relationship benefited us both. We both held a darkness from our past, a part of our humanity, that compromised our integrity and loyalty in self and each other. We both had experiences that threw us into the abyss, lashing out as one drowning lashes out to be saved by another. I will always love her and if she contacted me wanting to start anew, I would open myself to her, in my honest truth of who I am today, right now.

When one starts or ends a relationship, the act isn't necessarily bad or wrong. Sometimes it comes from deep grief, like with me and my friend. Sometimes it comes from a place of unconditional love. Life is less about being right or wrong, good or bad, and more about being mutually respectful, considerate, mindful, and kind. Life is about reciprocity. What we offer ourselves is a full well from which to offer to others. What we give, we receive. What we allow ourselves to receive replenishes our wellspring. Sometimes the wellspring is steeped in the darkness of one's grief, thus the darkness of grief is at the core of the beginning and ending of relationships. The darkness is our humanity, the learned perception that drives the train of decisions. Sometimes new relationships are started in spite of what the world informs as good or bad for one's psyche and overall health. Some transitions of relationships are needed, like a season helps one to transition. Some endings are with the realization that the relationship is keeping them both small. The smallness revealed is the truth of what is keeping one hidden in the secrets of their darkness.

I decided to start a relationship with my now ex-husband five months after John's ascension. There is a strong suggestion in the psychological field that one shouldn't start such a relationship so soon after an experience so traumatic as one's child ascending. Looking back, I could hear my Soul shouting NO. However, my heart was shattered into a trillion pieces so fine it was like powder and that powder held no connection to my Soul. My heart was deaf to everything but one thing: helping my soon-to-be-husband become a father to his children and regain visitation with them. I was steeped in my own fear around not having my son in my physical realm and this became the darkness that was the driver for *saving* my fiancé and his boys from a life without each other. This became my entire "mission" at that point.

Prior to our marriage two years later, I was stationed in New Orleans for two months without him and almost decided not to go through with the wedding. I was getting those messages from Spirit again. Yet my psyche had convinced me that I was responsible for him and his children getting back together again. Again, I had to save myself from my own lion by perceiving I was saving him and his children from theirs. I was placing my own experience on them. I was using their challenges as my outlet to save my own life without my son in it. Even in my altruistic intentions, there was darkness at the core defining who I needed to be to feel like I had meaning and purpose. He did get visitation again, and his two boys and I had a mutually positive influence on each other. I needed to be needed and I saw a great need that needed to be given a chance. A chance I no longer had.

I continued to stay in that relationship after the children stopped communicating with him, again in the hopes that I could be the difference that brought them back together. I didn't awaken to my own truth until eight years after marrying him. The marriage had its benefits for me as well. I needed to feel needed, and I needed a partner. We both needed a partner in that time of our lives. We both were enablers to and for each other in our different darknesses. Now we are both happier, freer to live the lives we are now living without that relationship hindering us and keeping us small.

Avoidances as an Impact are diverse and hold relatable energies for each relationship. Some people avoid because they don't know how to be around one who is experiencing something they also hold a fear for. They feel too close to a truth that could also be one they might experience. The unknown is very scary. In their fear they don't know what to say or how to say it, so they avoid instead. They aren't being like this out of malicious intent, they just have never been confronted with this depth of travesty in their own lives and haven't learned how to respond. They will say things that don't make sense. Some will lash out in their fear. I once had a family member tell me that I was jealous because her child was still alive and mine wasn't. Yes, that hurt me deeply AND after I left her and gave myself time to breathe through the comment, I realized she was afraid, and her fear was the darkness that caused her to lash out. Some will laugh when it's not appropriate or tell jokes that aren't appropriate. These responses are all psychological forms used as outlets for feelings and emotions that have never been experienced before. In the psychology field, recognition that people tend to learn more from that which brings them pain rather than joy prevails as human nature. These responses are not okay and it's okay to say so and be heard.

Some people will simply drift away because the parent of an ascended child no longer "fits" into the group. Sometimes these parents are looked upon with pity. The parent doesn't need pity. They need people who don't step away because they don't want to fathom a life without their own child(ren). Lifestyles change because the lens that people now see through, both the ascended child's parent(s) and their closest friends and relatives, change. Some groups were the parents that stayed up all night playing games with the boys and made them fabulous snacks. They were the parents who created fun out of cardboard, pushing them down the hill when it snowed in July in Colorado or took them to the gym and showed them how to build the muscle they needed for sports. Now, as a parent whose child ascended, they aren't that lifestyle. If the children were super close, like my son and his friends, they stay in touch out of respect and memory for what everyone had and was in their bond. The parent of an ascended child not only loses the physical being of their own child, but they also lose the physical being of his/her closest friends. This is a very deep loss. I feel it is of great importance to recognize that this may occur, or perhaps it already is occurring. Whichever way a child's friends turn, it is okay and part of the healing process for both the parent of the ascended child and his friends. His friends are going through a very deep grief as well and their own grief places them in a deep cavernous abyss. It's important to share one's grief with those closest to self and their child so the "village" can heal as one, for all are in need of deep healing.

Individual relationships become group relationships as the village that heals all. It is when we share our grief that humanity learns how to share life and all life brings us. If we show others in our life the same seasonal transitions we are going through, this better helps them to understand the seasonal transitions they are and will go through in their own grief. Most of humanity doesn't allow themselves to feel their grief. Humanity has been taught to fear death and to treasure our youth. When a youth ascends, even if that youth is twenty-three or thirty-three years old, the fear that erupts within the survivors takes over, sometimes masking and negating opportunities to grieve in the fullness of one's self with others. The group becomes a community of family and friends and the members of the group reach out beyond the circle and invite others experiencing the same type of grief, and so the group grows into a larger community.

Avoidance darkens the path one traverses. Sharing in a safe space, like a group counsel circle, brings hope, and in hope light is shed on the darkness. The shape illuded to as a snake is revealed as simply a rope – a lifeline. When the community comes together as a circle of counsel and saves space for Spirit to enter, Spiritual healing takes place and opens the hearts of the grieving. The circle of counsel becomes the ceremonial act of ritual, reminding all who enter who they are. In re-membering all of who one is, one enters the peace that is beyond all understanding. In that peace, one feels and reunites Self to the love that offers them life again, and again.

SPIRITUAL IMPACTS

In re-membering all of one's self and experiencing the hope, peace, and love that is beyond all understanding, one enters an individual existential experience with Spirit. Spiritual transitions are transpersonal by their very nature and transcend us out of the smallness of our past as a result of our experience of traversing and transitioning through a living-death to an honored-life. Spirit takes us in one direction that removes us from the conscious mind of who we were, an ascension of faith in truth, and our Soul takes us on a journey of what Thomas Berry calls "inscendence," or journey into oneself, the wildness of our human earthy roots, as cited on page 23 in Plotkin's "*Soulcraft:Crossing into the Mysteries of Nature and Psyche.*" It is this inscendence that is the darkness of our human shadow work we sit with and befriend. It asks us to question everything we know and to know everything we question. It asks us to mean what we say and say what we mean. The inscendence path teaches us to learn the difference between definition and meaning, intention and purpose, journey and path, and how those differences aid us in revealing our newfound truth. It asks us to ask ourselves the deeper question of who we are, without the social, economic, political, and religious labels and definitions that structure our personality from who we were to who we are to who we will become. The path asks us to willingly strip ourselves naked and dig in the earth with only our raw hands to uncover the gems of our truth. The path asks us to enter into a human development of Ego Growth to Soul Embodiment, to Spirit Realization (Plotkin, 2003, pg. 31) as we step onto each steppingstone of our journey. For each stone holds its own development for one's spiritual journey, impacted by a living-death.

During the initial impact of my living-death, I clung to the love that held me close prior to my son's ascension. Spirit showed me what They felt when Jesus ascended. For about seven to eight months The Divine had been sending me messages of what it was to feel, in every fiber of one's being, what They felt when Jesus accepted His destiny and ascended at the hands of others. As time went on, the feelings from those messages became more intense – so much so that I recall falling to my knees, asking Them for whom these messages were for and to help me when the time comes. I did not know They were sharing my own need that would come from my own child's ascension. John was my Heart and that heart would have no purpose for beating. I clung to that love and asked Jesus to help me breathe every breath needed so I wouldn't dishonor my son.

As time went on and I started writing my first book "Wo-Man" (which is under the pseudonym Eira Ashling Kynthia, with an edited version coming soon), which is a look at the divinity of women. I researched all the spiritual passages I cited so I could share the original format and thus the origin of meaning, rather than what those passages have come to mean as controls over others. My faith was tested, and I was asked by Spirit to question what I thought I knew as truth and to question the basis of my own relationship with Them. One's faith is an existential journey that is experienced through verifying, not accepting through a belief system. To verify one's own faith is a quest seeking one's own mystical gnosis, not another's. In my journey traversing my living-death and finding a way to emerge to an honored-life, I began to seek truth as a deeper, more personal relationship with The Divine. I found shocking records that gave me pause and caused me to question the foundations of the Christian faith. I felt as if I were in the same desert that Jesus traveled through, being tested in the darkness that was my abyss. When I began to live by an eco-theological understanding of the passages of The Word, I began to see Jesus and His teachings in a new light through a different colored lens.

My journey from a living-death to an honored-life impacted my spiritual path more than any other. I went from what I thought was a rich and fulfilling, albeit dualistic relationship with God as a father figure, to a rebellious and absent accord, to an empirical relationship with The Divine as the trinity of Father, Mother, and Son. For me, ceremonies have brought me full circle, transitioning from a dualistic, fearful supplication to a reverent service. A service for Self in who I am and who I am to become with Spirit. I have come to recognize that ceremonies of reverent service are transitional in nature, not a passive act of supplication – a way to communicate what is in my heart that words can't express. Ceremony aids one in verifying their faith through the ritual and the ritual becomes a lifestyle of noble faith. One becomes the inner illumination of The Divine and offers that illumination as a gift to the world. In my quest for truth, I learned that Jesus was the greatest shaman to show us what the inner illumination looks, feels, sounds, tastes, and smells like as Spirit in the world around us. His teachings are the essence of Saint Francis of Assisi's life and Saint Francis led others to live by.

Since my teen years, I know that who I choose to be is the essence, the basis, the root of who I am. The psychology and ecopsychology studies have broadened the lens through which I see life and opened myself up, with heart, mind, and soul, to engage with who I am and who I am becoming. How I choose to show up is the basis of the theological roots which cultivate the essence of my Self so that the fruit that is bared to the world can serve the world – human and non-human alike.

I offer a poem that has been relevant to the Spirit's still, small voice that is my guide on my journey. That still, small voice that asks me to descend on my inscendence path, with a cuppa or a shot, and befriend my own darkness until I see the light it holds. It is a poem of reflection and a knock on the door, inviting me to ask my Self (Soul) the why questions until I find the gems hidden there so that I may live life again in honor and grace for self and my son.

Sweet Darkness
…Time to go into the dark
where the night has eyes
to recognize its own.

There you can be sure
you are not beyond love.

The dark will be your womb
tonight.

The night will give you a horizon
further than you can see.

You must learn one thing.
The world was made to be free in you.

Give up all the other worlds
except to the one which you belong.

*Sometimes it takes darkness and the sweet
confinement of your aloneness
to learn*

*anything or anyone
that does not bring you alive*

is too small for you.

— David Whyte

CONSIDERATIONS
FOR
SUPPORTERS

*Your instinct may be to avoid someone who is experiencing loss
because you fear you'll say the wrong thing.
But loss can be very isolating, and if you stay away,
you will compound the loss and the pain.*

—Robbie Miller Kaplan

A parent of an ascended child will never be the same, even if they have other children. The cord that connected them and their child in the physical world has been forever severed, each parent will experience the loss of that physical connection differently. What works for one parent won't necessarily work for another – and that's okay and normal. Parents also react to the various areas of their lives differently, including how they interact with their families and very close friends, as well as colleagues. It's important to not take their changes personally, for they are not. Their internal landscape is trying to survive the chaos that has destroyed all they have ever known. Their truth and all they ever believed in and thought was unquestionable has now been called into question. This is supposed to happen.

It is very important that supporters do not attempt to bring parents back to what they think is best. It is *extremely* important supporters don't take changes to spiritual and religious beliefs, practices, and faith as a "sin," "evil," "misguided," and/or try to shape or steer parents' beliefs. Each parent will explore all of that on their own and eventually conclude to what "feels" right and rite to them in their Soul. I abandoned all I was ever taught since my childhood about Christ and the Christian faith. Over time, however, I returned to what I knew was absolute truth about Christ and the Angels and my own interpretation of the Word, not what has been (and still is) taught by patriarchal governing institutions. I revealed for myself what my faith is, not what is expected of me.

Parents of ascended children will, at some point, abandon the expectations of others and what is socially, politically, economically, spiritually, religiously, ethnically, and culturally acceptable and expected of them. The Battalion Commander and Sergeant Major of the command I was serving in when my son ascended told me I should "Just get over it. Everyone has lost someone in their life." They then proceeded to badger and harass me during my physician-directed and Regional Command-approved leave until I was forced to report them to the Army General's Office and the Office of Medical Command. I had to abandon what was expected of me as a Soldier and be what was needed for me – mentally, emotionally, psychologically, and physically – after my son's ascension.

What I chose to be for myself during that time led me to report them to the higher commands over all of the Army. The higher commands heard my pleas and recommended changes based on my experience at the time. Through me being for me I was able to be a catalyst for change for the greater good of all Soldiers that experienced the ascension of a child, as well as the governing Army and Air Force medical regulations. Those who supported me during that time and need weren't even aware of their positive impact. Sometimes the support is helping the parent overcome and be stronger for it just by following the parent's lead. Sometimes the support is just being there in the same room, or just listening, or being a shoulder, or cooking, or caring for other children in their household, or running errands, or getting them out. There is never a wrong form of support when the support is viewed from the parent's need and not the supporter's. Answering the call of what is needed is the answer to their call, even when one doesn't know what they are calling for and/or the supporter doesn't know the answer. Just showing up IS the answer – physically or on the phone.

It's okay to not have the answers or know the call, for, as mentioned, each circumstance is experienced differently by all involved and no two will walk the same path or in the same waters of grief. Tempers and patience will be tried in the hearts and minds of both the parent and the supporter. Again, that's okay, as long as loving understanding follows. It's important to remember that blame is self-inflicted in grief because one feels hopeless and helpless to change the situation. It's human nature to find an outlet for the stages that grief shows up in. Many say grief holds five or six stages. I agree with the stages and add that each stage also holds within it the four seasons that transition us from one stage to another for as many times as needed. Sometimes those stages internally "flare up" when one is in deep grief and an outlet is required. Unfortunately, the outlet sought out is often not a peaceful one. Just know that the parent isn't lashing out at the supporter; it's at the darkness one is experiencing and who the parent is in that darkness. The darkness is a formidable opponent for a parent whose child has ascended.

While this is largely a psychological struggle, with them grasping for help as they feel themselves descending further into the abyss of their living-death, it is also a physical and spiritual struggle. That said, these struggles are not permission to be unkind toward supporters. Abusive, aggressive, and generally unkind behavior isn't okay. In fact, supporters of one who is grieving so deeply should be honored and given grace for the grief that is also unfolding in them. One does not grieve on an island of one, though there are many moments when it feels like this. It's okay to gently help a grieving parent also see the supporters as grievers. This depth of grief is new to everyone involved, and only through trial and error do they learn to acknowledge one another with mutual consideration and respect so loving understanding follows.

Support groups are best in facilitating that loving understanding between supporters and grieving parents. Such groups provide a space that assists members in seeing others' viewpoints so they are acknowledged and honored. Supporters can participate in the group's experiential activities with the grieving parent(s), and this is when all receive the greatest gifts of that activity. Sharing is more caring because empathy imbues the compassion of the experiences; the differences in those experiences are like the many facets of a prism revealing the collective beauty that is the group. Groups also offer different perspectives around when and how to speak, listen, see, touch, and respond.

Groups are a safe haven where the ritual of unveiling of one's truth in who they are in that moment is a ritual of noble witnessing for each other and one's Self. Within the circle they experience themselves transitioning through the various stages and thus come face-to-face with a Divine connection. That connection is then projected as forms of speaking, listening, seeing, touching, feeling, and responding. The interconnectedness of the group members as they become one manifests as synchronistic flow for Self and others. The seeds are planted through group cohesion, thus creating and cultivating a "garden" for all to harvest the delicious bounty for healing.

There are many types of groups and not all require talking. Communication comes in many forms, writing to drawing to singing to dancing to sewing to knitting to sand art. All of these forms are Divine in nature, for creation is an external act of the Soul, experienced in the seasonal transformation of Spring's seeding and cultivation of oneself. The art form that is released from within oneself is also sowed and harvested.

An example of one form of artistic release, sowed with Divine seeds and harvested for whole person well-being and health is sand art. I personally witnessed this as I watched the creation of a mandala with sand. This creation starts in the seeds (the gridlines drawn from the patient love seeded in the hearts of the participants). What emerges over time is the Summer's infant child in its intentions for Divine purpose as the sands are meticulously released in the awe and wonder of what is emerging. Patience and human physical discomfort, which shows up in the pain of bending over the table to create the mandala, signifies the seasonal transition from Summer's body into Fall's adolescent mind. What one in the group experiences so do all, thus, this transition moves into Winter's heart through community, raising each up to fulfill the task. Once the period of creating the mandala closes, the group ends with perhaps a prayer of gratitude for being of service to Spirit for the greater good of self, the group, and the gift given for all. Mental, emotional, and psychological healing takes place, which is then stored in the heart and mind, thus creating an abundant bounty of healing energy for the body and Soul. When one offers healing to their mental and emotional states, they offer and afford themselves a healing energy that opens the window of the heart and mind to see the love that offers them life again and again on their journey.

This reminded me of the bible passage when Jesus tells us to be in the world, not of the world. The creation of one's internal world is the mandala, for it was offered from the Divine. The swirl of recollecting the sands and releasing them into the wind after the mandala is created and photographed by the group is an act of being in the world, not being affected by the release of the sands. The sands were the offerings that create an external life, the mandala is a picture of that life. The swirls are an assimilation of the circumstances of a parent's life without their child's physical presence and what that parent sees as their living-death; releasing the sands into the wind is releasing the hold of grief. The more one can practice this ritual as their creative release, the more they are capable of living in the moment of what life creates for each of us in our journey, whether we are a parent or a supporter. With continued practice of creative release, one's heart and mind remember the healing stored, offering the bounty of healing created within one's inner landscape – and in their life outside of the creative format.

One can also choose to release the sands in a body of flowing water, like a river, stream, or creek. The release in the water is an offering to return the sands back from whence they came – back to The Divine – for we are born from living waters and return to the waters of life. The passage where Jesus tells us that from ashes we came and to ashes we return has held new meaning for me since John's ascension, as I have his ashes until I ascend and they are combined to be returned to our ancestral Celtic waters.

How will those who engage in creative release – be it sand art, painting, music, song, charcoal drawing, dance, sculpture, et cetera – choose to step out so that others may witness the ceremony within them? How will you, a parent of an ascended child, now choose to step out as a witness for your child's life within? How will you, as a supporter, reach out to walk beside that parent in sync with their flow of transitioning from one season to another, as they transcend from who they were to who they are and to become? Like the sands released from the art created, the art format transitioning from what was to what is to what will become is the transition of parent and supporter to who they were. to who they are, into who they will become in their own truth.

What follows are some areas that are impacted in one's being within and from their transitioning from a living-death to an honored-life. I hope these areas add the clarity I gained when thinking upon them for myself.

To Speak or Not to Speak

Know that one won't always have the answers and/or words that convey their love and support for a grieving parent. When words are shared, it's important to remember that the relationship is a two-way form of communication. In Naropa council circles we all sat facing each other on fluffy meditation mats and pillows. There was always an empty meditation mat reserved for Spirit's presence in the group. During that group circle there were five rules, as described in Jack Zimmerman's book, "*Way of Council*," by which we followed:

1. Basic Set-up: Don't speak out of turn. The one with the talking piece is the one given the honor and respect to speak what is in them until they pass the talking piece to the next person.

2. Speak from the heart. If it isn't kind, helpful, or absolutely necessary to assist another with their own inquiry then it isn't from the heart. The heart holds and offers compassion and empathy, which are the touchstones by which thoughts are conveyed into words.

3. Listen from the heart. The act of listening from the heart is an act of mutual reciprocity that offers each a safe space to be heard, seen, and recognized without judgement, condemnation, or shame.

4. Speak from a place of spontaneity. When one is truly listening to another, they aren't allowing their mind to wander and wonder what their response will be to the one they are supposed to be listening to. When one listens from the heart, one sees and hears what another can't or won't say. A response to another is then from the heart without rehearsal.

5. Be brief. When speaking, it takes a lot of attention from others to hear what is being said and not said and to see the person in how they are expressing themselves. Attention to detail tires one out and shortens one's attention span. Brevity aids comprehension.

When words can't convey or aren't needed, silence speaks volumes and sometimes is very loud. Silence allows one to fully see who another is in that moment, as silence requires sight to infer and inform. Silence holds its own fascinating and enchanting energy. The world is so noisy with its demands that our minds require silence to enable us to recognize self and others. Silence is almost always comforted with the slightest touch. A hug isn't always needed or required. There is great healing in silence while holding one's hand. At the end of this chapter there are three experiential activities around silence and the powerful grace in love that silence holds.

To Touch or Not to Touch

Know that touch isn't always necessary and sometimes touch is the healing element. The grieving parent is absent of their child and may just need to curl up like a baby in the womb, for this is where they are in their heart, in that moment. They are in the Season of darkness. This can occur months or years later, for grief does not have an on/off switch – it just is, at different degrees and intensities. A parent can't touch their child and may change their natural instincts for touch. Those who are naturally touchy-feely people may display the inability to touch their child in their posture. If someone stiffens, crosses their arms over their torso, creates distance between themselves and others, or hugs their knees or an inanimate object (like a throw pillow), that person is sending signals that they don't want to be touched in that moment. It's important to respect that space they are needing. On the other hand, those who are known to avoid touch may be drawn to those supporters who are touchy. In either case, watching for the cues and inquiring if confused is always thoughtful. Touchstones are a wonderful tool that offers encouragement, rest in distressful times, and soothing comfort when one is alone and needs touch. I encourage each supporter to get for themselves and the one they support a touchstone that they can carry in their pocket or place beside their bed or favorite chair.

Psychologically, physical touchstones are used to assist one during a traumatic event and the relationship of Self with that event. Think of a favorite stuffed toy or blanket that a child reaches for when they are upset and how that toy or blanket comforts them. This same comfort can be received from rubbing a touchstone. Every time one picks up a touchstone, the very movement of the finger or thumb rubbing it sends soothing messages to the brain and opens the cognitive centers for deeper understanding of oneself in relation to the event. A journal also assists one to convey one's thoughts on that relationship and the relativity of oneself to the event in that moment. A weighted blanket is another form of a touchstone. I use one at night to help me sleep sounder and I don't wake up in a panic attack. As mentioned earlier, panic attacks are my body's way of remembering what it feels like to die, as I died twice as a small child from pneumonia. My body also relates those memories to the reality of my son's death, so I, in essence, feel his death as a very real event in my body. The weighted blanket offers me the gift of being held and opens the cognitive centers to the soothing comfort being held brings. Because the cognitive centers are receiving positive reinforcement from the body, the mind sends mirroring chemicals to the body that offer comfort, not the memories of what death feels like.

Food, like rain, is a reciprocal touchstone that offers nourishment and healing for the greater good of all. Bringing food to a grieving parent, especially if they have other children, offering to cook for them, or sharing the cooking journey with them and/or their children is one of the best gifts one can offer as a form of communication. My mom always said food comes from The Divine and love is cooked in. In bringing food, even if it's from a restaurant, or cooking for another, one offers that love from The Divine through them and their mindfulness of another. The relationship between a grieving parent and food is that they see themselves as needing, and receiving, the care of community. It doesn't only require a village to raise a child, it requires a village to nourish one through grief. As one experiencing a living-death and seeking emergence from the abyss, the Season of Emergence is the child needing the village. The joy the village receives when the child emerges from her living-death and continues to transition through the seasons to an honored-life, comes from witnessing how their care and comfort helped nourish her back to a love that brings her back to life, again and again.

The Healing Wall

The Healing Wall in Jerusalem is a form of touchstone as well. The wall has holes in it that people place their prayers in for Yahweh's intervention. Most then go on about their business, failing to participate in their own request to The Divine. There is a story that many have probably heard that is the epitome of spiritual bypassing, where we leave everything in our prayers up to God and fail to participate in our part for that prayer to be realized. The paradigm is thus:

A hurricane occurred in a small town and the water started to rise. A man ran out of his house and prayed to God to save him. A bus came with all kinds of people from different areas of the city. The driver told the man to get in so they could take him to shelter. He thought others could use the bus more so than him and so declined, saying that God would save him. The water rose and he fled to the second story of his home. He prayed again to God to save him from the rising water. A boat from the Coastguard arrived and told him to get in. The boat was filling up fast with people and he feared it would tip over. He didn't know how to swim and so he told them no, that God would save him. The water continued to rise and he got on top of his roof and prayed and prayed for God to save him. A helicopter came and told him to get in the harness so they could pull him in and he declined, afraid of falling out of the harness. He prayed, shaking his fists and asking why God wasn't saving him. An Angel appeared and told the man that God had sent him saving grace three times, and because he feared something from each form sent, he failed to see that God was saving him.

Sometimes help comes in unexpected ways and one simply needs to stop wailing at the wall for fear that they will bother someone else, or out of guilt for not permitting oneself to be mired in grief 24/7, or anger because all the people they pushed away no longer contact them, or fear of the form the savior takes. These forms of fear and grief are one's own anguish they pour out on the wall and the wall is what one creates in their inner landscape to shelter themselves from being seen, in their truth, by others. The wall is their stoicism, and the stoicism the resistance to the saving grace that is freely given by others. One wails at the wall they perceive as blocking them from receiving the answers and guidance they say they need, not realizing they created that wall through bypassing what and who Spirit sent them. In Jungian psychology one learns that one creates their own dilemma through their willingness to participate in the dilemma. This is the shadow side of one's wailing wall.

On the other side of that wailing wall is where light appears to reveal how one can begin to tear down the wall that has kept one in a state of relentless wailing. When one prays for assistance in coping and moving through the moments of their grief, they simply need only touch their heart. Meditation is a form that allows one to listen to Spirit so the heart can be touched by the love that offers one a life filled with hope, not wailing grief. The heart sends signals of what is one's truth in that moment. Be in that truth and allow the wailing to be realized in real-time and let the tears flow. Allow oneself to be seen through the tears. Tears reveal the flooding of the emotions that sends one to the roof as the emotions rise. The tears then become another touchstone. Even the Universe uses tears as her touchstone, releasing that which becomes too burdensome to carry any longer. To release one's grieving burden is to nourish not only the soul grieving but to nourish the souls of those witnessing, for allowing one to be witnessed in all their truth is a gift to the witness as well. As the clouds release rain as nourishment for the greater good of all and become more spacious and open to receive, so does one who permits themselves to be seen in their tears. Like nature's exchange, so is the exchange between the fullness of grief in tears and expansion to receive nourishment from witnesses in their release. It's the reciprocal life force of ebb and flow.

Tears aren't a sign of weakness; they are a bold and courageous display of what is alive inside a grieving heart. I spoke earlier of the heart and the heart's neuro centrum and how the heart sends and stores messages and memories in the body. The heart is the center of one's life force and how one feels the energies of the world internally and externally. Tears are a gift that expands one's heart and opens one to receive the healing touch of others. As supporters, that healing touch can appear to them as well in the witnessing, allowing themselves to be witnessed in their own tears. In denying oneself this rescuing gift, be they a parent or a supporter, they are stifling the life energy that seeks the remedy for their dilemma. Stoicism is not heroic. One can never hope to move forward in a life well-lived, in honor of self and their child, or another, if their life force is not permitted to ebb and flow. Think of a still pond that has no inlet or outlet. The pond becomes putrid and what life was in it soon dies. Grief is the inlet and tears are the outlet.

Time Waits Not for One's Fullness

The wailing wall is not the only block that one burdens themselves within their grief. Time can be perceived as either a gift or a burden. When one thinks of time as linear, it then can become the latter. There is a book by Dr. Seuss titled *Oh the Places You'll Go!* that I give to graduates – it is a gift that continues to give to them as they rise to their fullest potential. In that book there is a passage around time and waiting. There is a waiting place and in this waiting place one is to seek inside, to ponder who they are and where they will go, what they learned, and all that they will explore along the way. This waiting place is eternal, asking us to consider these questions with every experience.

Grief isn't a time of just waiting. It is a time for one to ponder who they are in that moment of grief, what they are learning about themselves, where they need to go to transition from their current state to a higher potential of honored-life, and all that they are offering themselves and those who witness them where they will go next to honor their child's life within their own. This is true for supporters as well, for supporters also grieve. The waiting place is eternal in the journey of the Soul experiencing what it is to be human. It is a place to visit for a short period so that one can transition through the human experience. The waiting place is the place where one sits with their darkness and shares a cuppa or a shot so that revelations and wisdom may be received from their darkness. The revelations offer touchstones of wisdom within the touchstone of the moment in time.

Allow time to be a touchstone, seeing it as the waiting place of reflection so that one can move from one experience to another. Viewing time as such allows one to dance once again. I heard a saying the other day: "Change one's stance to change the dance and the dance will change one's stance." In this stance, one embraces the time given to be kinder, gentler, more compassionate and honoring of one's journey, instead of avoiding the time given for and to the journey. Time is not linear, for when we transition through a time of seasons, we are offered the gift to transition again with greater potential for oneself. Time no longer appears to be a burden in the waiting place, and the waiting place becomes a place of reflection toward a more inspired honored-life. What one needs to spend time with is there, in the waiting, and in the waiting place is found peace for transitioning in a love that brings one back to life again and again.

FINDING PEACE

Peace.
Peace is a sacred garment
softened by the eternal solitude of silence.
Silence is the heart of God.
A promise that we are never, ever alone.

—James Allen

The hope of a peace found in the Divine's ethereal state of peace, that peace that goes beyond all understanding, is cultivated through ritual and ceremony found in the four stages of the wheel of life we all pass through – consciously and unconsciously. Recognizing how the transition from each stage in the seasons frees us of the pain and suffering of who we were, into who we are, emerging into who we will become, is the gift of peace. It is a promise of a love that shows us how to live again, and again. A promise of a love that serves one's Self as the rituals begin to communicate to them what is in their heart. An active, daily ritual I have come to engage in without fail is to make morning tea in an antique silver teapot, watching the water pour onto the loose tea leaves as it transforms those dried leaves into a golden liquid that nourishes my body, mind, and heart in so many ways. After I sit with my tea, I close my eyes and offer a short humming of gratitude and Lucia, my first therapy kitty, jumps in my lap and rests. The silence that follows, and Lucia's presence, is The Divine sharing their physical presence of love and care for me. The silence of the tea ritual is a time to be in the silent promise. A promise that I am only alone when I fail to remember that I am in the presence of my son, for he lives in me. I am his legacy, as he is mine. I remember because I offer myself the ritual every day.

Each parent of an ascended child *is* the legacy of their child, not the other way around, for as they choose to live in honor of their child and their child's gifts, the parent becomes their child's living embodiment. Every step a parent takes as new babes in the wonder and awe of their season of emergence is a step into the unknown of who they each are becoming. Begin at the beginning and be reborn, as a babe entering into the unknown, exploring all the senses the Soul seeks in her experience as a human. Enter your transition and discover your truth for you now. Become, and know that you are a child of the Divine, stepping out in the promise of your child's legacy through you.

Every day we are given the opportunity to be reborn, to step out and choose differently. I offer you the opportunity to choose differently by choosing yourself. To choose your Self within the dawnings and awakenings found within the pages of this book. In choosing your Self, your higher Self, you choose your child who still lives within you, giving you back your purpose in life, for life, with the life of your child. We are the legacy of their ancestral heritage. We are their Spiritual Season in our humanness. We are the breath of life, found in the love, so deep and so nourishing, the only hope that remains for each of us is the ritual of our life for our children. Step out and emerge, again and again, in the ritual of love that offers you life, again and again.

OFFERINGS

Complimentary Pamphlet

When you purchase the book from my website you will be sent a complimentary, electronic version of *Elements of the Four Seasons and Their Transitions* pamphlet I created for understanding the seasons within oneself more deeply. If you have purchased this book from a bookstore, please go to my website at https://cynthiaeyer.kartra.com/page/home to receive your complimentary e-pamphlet. It is my gift to you in gratitude for trusting me with your transitions from your Living-Death to your Honored-Life. A life lived in honor of yourself, your child, and the life you shared. A life being lived as a living ritual of who your child still is, through you.

Life Journal

Coming soon there will be an offering of a *Life Journal* and a live group counsel that will meet to journey through the seasons and stages of the wheel for a set period of time. The times and period are to be determined, so be sure to connect with me on the website at https://cynthiaeyer. kartra.com/page/home and sign up for email notifications of this promising event. Groups are collective ceremonial times that offer reverent service so all can communicate what is in the heart that words cannot always express. Experiences are shared, offering deeper aid in moving through each transformational stage found for self and each member of the group. The group is a physical, living promise that none are alone. This group will become the visual experience of the inner illumination of each child, shared and experienced through each parent in the group. The group is both an individual and collective quest for truth to enable all to experience their journey from a living-death to an honored-life more fully. The journal will offer many more experiential activities to further each parent's and supporter's journey to who they are becoming, as well as space to write out their experience. Writing out one's experience is an act of self-reflection that offers greater understanding. Writing is a form of sitting with a cuppa and befriending the darkness, gleaming the precious jewels one's darkness holds.

Other Readings – Books listed in the Bibliography are excellent additional sources to assist one in their journey from living-death to honored-life after the ascension of their child. Parents will go through their journey in different ways, through the stages of the seasonal wheel of life at different times in their life, for the rest of their life. The journey of a parent of an ascended child is the most difficult, most sorrowful journey one can traverse. This level of sorrow is why it is so important to gain as much understanding as one needs and desires as tools for their journey. Even after nineteen years, I still witness each of these seasonal stages in the transformational experiences when I reach for the tools shared in this book. Each time I gain a deeper, more significant gnosis of my son's life within me. Each transformation is a stepping stone; thus, each stone becomes the rock by which one finds their grounding so they may move to the next. I hope you find as much healing in the understanding of seasonal stages as I have through these additional readings that accompany the spiritual oneness one possesses and experiences with their child in the inevitable seasonal transformations.

Touch Stones

Touchstones can be any physical object that you can touch or carry in your pocket. A touchstone can be an altar or an object on the altar, a smooth stone (with or without a word or symbol on it), a devotional book or a tarot deck (both hold messages from Spirit), a religious symbol such as a cairn or cross in a beautiful/healing setting, or a favorite book or movie, to name just a few.

TERMINOLOGY

The Divine – My concept of God/Jehovah/The Universe/Creator/One/Lord-Goddess/Spirit/Them/One Who Shall Not Be Named as the creator of the universe. The Divine embraces both masculine and feminine qualities, thus benefitting our world and all creation within and in support of all life with both masculine and feminine qualities. The Divine is All as One and One as All. The Divine is the "I AM" of Who we are in our higher truth – our Soul.

Ecopsychology – A psychological modality by which one's analysis of one's life is viewed as a relationship between the human self and the non-human environment. Inter-relational, psychological theories and research methodologies assist us in the awareness of how our outward external landscapes in the natural environment are guides to our own internal landscapes in mind, psyche, body, heart, and soul. Transpersonal Ecopsychology also involves growing an awareness of who one is and one's own truth beyond social and governmental constructs that have colonized the masses to believe, from institutional perspectives, who one is supposed to be.

Transformational Seasons – One's life is best described as seasonal transformations. As the external seasons transition and transform the external landscapes, so do the internal seasonal transitions and transformations of one's mind, psyche, heart, body, and soul transform the external land-scapes of our life, in the form of our choices. Who one is, and is becoming, is a product and reflection of one's environment and vice versus.

Liminal Space – The space in between the seasonal transitions and trans-formations, both internally and externally. The space that is all things at once and nothing at all, as it is the space between one door shutting, or already shut, and one door yet to open. It is the darkness that is the space between rooms in the mansion we have been promised by The Divine and have forgotten we live in.

Transcendental – Relates to a spiritual and/or non-physical/ethereal experience that brings one to a greater awareness of Self – the higher Self, the Soul's connection with the Divine. Transcendence is an emergence into a higher vibrating state of whole being. The higher the vibrations the more open one becomes to witnessing the vibrations of one's ascended child/other that exists as living vibrations within Self.

BIBLIOGRAPHY

Andren, Grace (2018). *Speaking in Tears: The poetry of grief.* AnCor Press.

Braden, Gregg (2020, April 12). *The Ancient Technique To Making Tough Decisions.*
https://www.youtube.com/watch?v=exHp3L_c2Lg

Foster, Stephen & Little, Meredith (1999). *The Four Seasons: The initiatory seasons of human nature.* Lost Borders Press.

Kessler, David (2019). *Finding Meaning: The sixth stage of grief.* Scribner.

Kolk, Bessel van der (2015). *The Body Keeps the Score: Brain, Mind, and Body in the Trauma of Healing.* Penguin Books.

Lane, Beldon C. (1998). *The Solace of Fierce Landscapes: Exploring Desert and Mountain Spirituality.* Oxford University Press.

Plotkin, Bill (2003). *Soulcraft: Crossing into the Mysteries of Nature and Psyche.* New World Library.

Singer, Michael A. (2007). *The Untethered Soul: The Journey Beyond Yourself.* New Harbinger Publications, Inc.

Watterson, Megan (2019). *Mary Magdalene Revealed.* Hay House Publishing, *Inc.*

Zimmerman, Jack & Coyle, Virginia (1996). *Way of Council.* Bramble Books.

ABOUT THE AUTHOR

Cynthia Eyer is a catalyst for change as she strives to be the difference for the greater good of all. As a single parent of her only-child who has ascended, she saw herself as losing her motherhood, legacy and purpose for life. She reveals how the unique approach of utilizing the four seasons as guides becomes the introspection by which each parent gains the confidence, skills, and hope to traverse the abyss of their grief and emerge into the wholeness of a more profound life of honor that is entwined with their child's shared legacy to their own. She shares the stories of her journey through the seasons from her living-death to an honored-life as a Universal Mother, midwifing the birth of seasonal transitions mothers and fathers are experiencing in their own journeys. As an Ecopsychologist, Spiritual Coach, and Army Mortuary Affairs Consultant, Cynthia gently guides parents within and through their seasonal transitions and the impacts of that journey as a sacred, ritualistic practice that grounds them in the love shared with their child: the love that transcends death into life again and again.

ACKNOWLEDGMENTS

To the three remaining of the Four Amigos, Jimmy, Jeremiah, and Ryan.
Thank you for allowing me to continue to see my son through your lives
and for your continued support.
I am still a "Mom" because of your love.

CJ and Mr. Joe.
I am immeasurably grateful for you both as John's "Brothers."
He is so proud of you both, as I am, and smiles as
he watches your families grow in such an unwavering love.

To my many "Sisters" who have supported, mentored, and guided me
through these last almost 20 years (You know who you are).
You have been my "Village."

To Thomas, Blair, Christopher, and Mikey,
I love you to the moon and back several times.
You opened your home and your hearts
when I needed it the most and never wavered in your loving care for me.
I Bow to you and am ever grateful you are my family.

To Justin
You honor me by naming your son, Shawn, with my son's middle name.
No words can express my joy in you and your family.

To the Transcendent Publishing Team
This Memoir would not be possible without
your advisorship and guidance in its journey from a
seed into what it is and will become.